LEO VAN WITSEN

Costuming for
OPERA

Who Wears What and Why

Volume II

The Scarecrow Press, Inc.
Metuchen, N.J., & London
1994

First published by Indiana University Press, Bloomington, Indiana, 1981.

British Library Cataloguing-in-Publication data available

Library of Congress Cataloging-in-Publication Data

Van Witsen, Leo, 1912–
    Costuming for opera : who wears what and why / by Leo
Van Witsen.
        p.   cm.
    Vol. 1 previously published: Bloomington : Indiana Uni-
versity Press, c1981.
    Includes bibliographical references and indexes.
    ISBN 0-8108-2744-1 (set). — ISBN 0-8108-2933-9 (v.1)
— ISBN 0-8108-2743-3 (v. 2) (acid-free paper)
    1. Operas—Stage guides.   2. Costume.   3. Opera—
Production and direction.   I. Title.
MT955.V36   1994
792.5'026—dc20   93-29999

CONTENTS

iv • *Costuming for Opera*

FOREWORD

*I*N THE THIRD SCENE of the fourth act of Shakespeare's The Taming of the Shrew, the Tailor quite innocently says:

> You bid me make it orderly and well,
> According to the fashion and the time.

How often during my years as head of the New York City Opera and during my opera conducting career in general, have I looked up at the costumes 'gracing' the stage and wished that the costume designer had followed the simple guidelines set forth by Shakespeare's Tailor. For the casual opera-goer the costumes are merely part of the decoration. Yet first-rate costuming is truly an art, and when it comes to the art of costume designing for opera, that art should be elevated to true beauty tempered only by basic functionality.

First, costume designers must make their designs fit in with the scenic designs, while being distinctive and interesting enough to help each character establish his or her personality. Once again it is Shakespeare who reminds us in Hamlet, "The apparel oft proclaims the man." By extension, the costumes in an opera production must also proclaim the character. Further, the costumer must have a deep sensitivity to the music so that the costumes do not clash with the music being heard. In essence the visual and auditory senses of the opera-goer must be approached as a unit since there is only one brain putting together the 'heard' and 'seen' images. (Unfortunately, even the most stunning costume cannot trick the listener into believing that an ugly voice is beautiful!) By the same token opera conductors should be sensitive to all the visual elements of a production. If they are not, it becomes very difficult to give a complete representation of the composer's vision to the audience, regardless of how musically perfect it may be.

We can be quite certain that in earlier times, when composers often served as conductors for their own operas, they were very involved in all the aspects of a performance, musical as well as visual. In this way they were better able to protect their work from interpretive license taken by the nonmusical forces.

Unfortunately, the swing of the pendulum has brought us the excesses which nowadays disgrace so many opera stages throughout the world. Far too often the stage pictures bear little or no relation to the composer's intention and thus there is no way for music and design to provide a unified image. Incongruous costuming assaults the audience's senses, and while there are those who believe that it is necessary to jar today's operagoing public I, for one, believe that in most cases the composer's wishes and original concept must be followed. If we believe that great composers craft great operas, then the random updating under the guise of 'pertinence' which has become the rage is truly out of place, or more precisely, out of time. The true artists among scenic and costume designers are those who can be wonderfully imaginative, yet manage to keep their creativity in check for the good of the overall production.

What must costume designers deal with in their efforts to combine the fantasy of the stage with the reality of performance? First they must keep their artistic desires in check in order to accommodate the mundane: practicality. An opera costume must be functional. For example, a cowl which covers the singer's ears making it difficult to hear the orchestra and the other singers, poses obvious problems. Further, the designer must consider the stage business each character must perform. If, for example, Cherubino in Act II of *The Marriage of Figaro* is required to jump out of the Countess' window, the costume must allow the performer to do so with speed and ease; thus a long cape or other encumbrances over Cherubino's basic outfit, would be unworkable.

Another important consideration for the costume designer is the quick costume change. Very often a singer must change costumes in a matter of a very few moments. If the design does not take that into account, the singer may miss his or her next entrance. Finally, the fabrics chosen must give the singers the comfort they need to perform their best. Heavy materials, though they may add a nice visual effect, are usually cumbersome and unkind under the hot lights of the stage.

These are just some of the elements an opera costume designer needs to consider. Once these basic strictures are observed the designer then should consider the opera's setting, time, and place; a sixteenth-century Pilgrim's costume would not seem quite right in Count Almaviva's castle in eighteenth-century Spain! Nonetheless in this age of the 'stage director' even good designers often have difficulty asserting their knowledge of history and tradition. At last, once the basic approach has been agreed upon and the many problems, political as well as practical, have been settled, the costume designer is free to use all his or her creativity with colors, styles, and fabrics for the purpose of making the costumes blend and yet stand out.

Opera costuming is a complex task requiring a profound sensitivity to the music, fidelity to time and place, and severe practicality—all combined with a creative spirit. Oh how easy that sounds and how difficult it really is. Try to keep all that in mind as you read this fascinating book. And next time you are at the opera think of Canio in *Pagliacci,* who sings the immortal line: ''Vesti la giubba'' (Put on the costume) and remember what went into the design of that costume.

Julius Rudel

ACKNOWLEDGMENTS

*T*O MY FRIEND JULIUS RUDEL I am deeply indebted for writing the Foreword to this Volume. I was well aware that as an opera conductor his interests go well beyond the opera's musical aspects. That he is equally well versed in Shakespeare I would never have guessed. Thank you Julius!

The friends whose advice and assistance proved so valuable in the realization of this book's first volume, have persisted in their efforts for Volume II. Foremost among them are my longtime companion Robert Hess, and my opera-mentor Boris Goldovsky. Both were at all times ready to have their brains picked, and were equally eager to show me the errors of my ways.

My colleagues and friends Dean Brown, Steven Feldman, and David Roberts helped in deciding which fifteen operas to select as subject matter for this volume.

Robert Kaufman, the Associate Librarian of the Costume Library of the Metropolitan Museum of Art and his staff were ever ready to assist in my arduous search for suitable illustrations. Janet Bookspan shared her Japanese expertise for the *Butterfly* chapter and Robert T. Jones, the translator of many Janacek operas, did the same for the chapter on *Jenufa*. In Paris, David Baumunk leafed through an endless number of turn-of-the century French newspapers in order to discover what Parisian stevedores wore in 1910. Francesca Moban drew three illustrations. Colleague Peter J. Hall and Richard Wagner, head of the Metropolitan Opera's tailor-shop, permitted me to browse through the former's *Lohengrin* sketches for the Met's production of that opera.

Others who have given valuable advice were Robert Erler, Dr. Burton Hoffmann, Arthur Schoep, Dean Schwaab, Victoria Tanner, Maurits Van Witsen, and Prof. Frank White. I owe them all a debt of gratitude, and to those I forgot to mention, I owe a plea of mercy.

INTRODUCTION: THE COSTUME DESIGNER'S FUNCTION

*I*N THE REALM OF OPERA it is absolutely essential that those entrusted with the creation of a production's visual aspects are sensitive to music in the sense that listening to it conjures up visual imagery. Those who do not possess that gift, whose mind's eye does not respond to the sound of music, are well advised to shun creative involvement with the visual aspects of musical theatre.

Within the triumvirate that constitute the Stage Director's expert extensions: the Scene Designer, the Costume Designer, and the Lighting Designer, the role of the costume designer must on the surface seem self-evident. Closer investigation will prove it to be not quite so evident as all that.

When a designer is commissioned to conceive the costumes for a given opera, the following steps must be taken: Listen to the music and thus perceive an image of the opera's visual aspects. Next, compare the period in which the music was composed with the libretto's historical data, and reconcile the two. Not only has music a strong period flavor of its own, but at the time the opera was composed conventions in stage production may have existed which should be taken into account. Reading the original story on which the opera's libretto is based is the next important step to be taken. Because an opera libretto is merely a skeleton which the music fleshes out, much pertinent information and detail may be discovered in the original story, which the libretto of necessity omits. It is important to exercise good judgment in these matters. One may easily be seduced by fascinating details in the original story which have no bearing on the opera plot, have purposely been omitted, or have purposely been changed in the libretto.

After all this preliminary work, the costume designer can now proceed to conceive the attire for each individual role, bearing in mind the character's personality, age, social standing, the mood of each particular scene, and so forth. It must never be forgotten that a stage presentation is a 'tableau vivant,' wherein all the individual parts merge into a visual composition. That does not mean of course that some of its parts cannot stand out, as indeed in virtually all cases, they must.

As a component of the design triumvirate, costume designers are not independent agents. They must be willing and able to adjust their ideas to the concept laid out by the stage director. It was no different in my own case and with a few exceptions I was able to make the adjustment. Although, as a member of a theatrical costume establishment I was expected to satisfy the customers' wishes, I was allowed on a few occasions to relinquish an assignment which was artistically too much against my grain. Free-lance designers, whose commissions are often few and far between, might not find it so easy to reject an assignment which does not agree with their artistic convictions.

What separates costume designers from their scenic-and-lighting colleagues is the circumstance that their creations involve performers' bodies, and that opera singers, unlike legitimate actors, are much more emotionally vulnerable concerning the projection of their bodies on the stage. Like all people who are through circumstances forced to expose their person before an audience, they want to make a favorable impression and look beautiful in terms they understand. The terms they understand are the fashions of the day. That the art of singing involves the body to such a great extent, makes opera singers even more sensitive in that respect.

"The Age of the Prima Donna" is a thing of the past. Singers can no longer demand to wear on stage whatever pleases them regardless of what anyone else wears, and regardless of the designer's concept. By the same token performers are no longer permitted to provide their own wardrobe, which used to put matters entirely beyond the designer's control. In that respect I recall a new production at the Metropolitan Opera of *Les Contes D'Hoffmann,* which was set in the Empire period. Joan Sutherland who sang the roles of Olympia, Giulietta, and Antonia wore her own costumes, which were of the Rococo era. "I saved them a lot of money" the diva was quoted as saying. Today the stage-director rules the roost in that respect, and a singer who objects to the costumes assigned to him or her will be replaced. This is particularly true in Europe, and especially in Germany. I know successful performers who have relinquished their opera careers because of this, and at least one famous conductor whose objection to the stage-director's absolute rule induced him to cease conducting operas. I tend to be a little more philosophical about the present stage-directors' dictatorship. It is a fad, and like all fads: this too shall pass! Anyhow, it pertains only to productions that are conceived from scratch. In order to make these financially feasible, they are increasingly shared by several, at times as many as half a dozen, companies. In such cases the staff costume designers, who serve the individual companies, have their work cut out for them. Although productions may be shared, the casts are not. A costume that looked splendid on that tenor of great reknown in Cologne, where the production originated, may be a disaster on his famous colleague, who will interpret the role in San Francisco.

Designers aware of that situation, may be able to devise variations of their designs to suit the personalities and figures of various performers known to be cast in subsequent performances of that production. After all, within the budget of a total production, a few more principal costumes, costly though they may be, are not going to break the bank. It is the wardrobe for the vast numbers of choristers, dancers, and supernumeraries, (not to mention the elaborate sets, of course) that may cast opera producers into Chapter Eleven.

To what extent it is possible to create a costume that does justice to the many demands a role requires within the concept of the entire production and also consider the personality and figure of a specific interpreter, varies enormously with the level on which a given production was conceived. Oddly enough, the lower the level the better the chances. On a high level, let us say for the Metropolitan Opera Company in New York, the planning of a production as well as its casting, is done years in advance of the performances. As far as the casting is concerned, there is many a slip. . . . All opera-goers have received such slips inserted in their program, stating: 'at tonight's performance the role of such and such will be sung by so and so,' in contrast to the program's listing. We are all familiar with the emergence from the wings, of a gentleman, microphone in hand, who apprises the groaning audience, just prior to the curtain's rising, that a certain diva has succumbed to a sudden attack of malnutrition and will be unable to perform that evening. Luckily, another, uncertain diva has graciously consented to step in on short notice. She begs the audience's indulgence and will sing the part in her native tongue. Even if the costume designer were present at such an emergency, which is unlikely, unless it happens to be opening night, the costume problems occasioned by such a happenstance are dropped into the lap of the wardrobe personnel. Almost invariably these are experienced and capable artisans, thoroughly accustomed to such crises and able to cope with them. They also have the advantage of being familiar with the stock of costumes on hand, from which to select the ones that will fill the gap most satisfactorily. Yet the costumes the audience will behold on such an occasion, may of necessity be a far cry from what the designer intended.

Productions on a lower level constitute the bulk of what goes on in the opera world. The smaller the budget, the less money will be spent on costumes. What little there is will be allocated to scenery, while costumes may come almost as an afterthought. (Here speaketh the voice of experience!) Designing new costumes for the principals, while selecting everything else from rental stock, will be the first rung down the ladder. It is interesting to observe that according to the bylaws of the United Scenic Artists of America, the labor union to which all professional designers belong, selecting costumes from rental stock is considered designing, and on an equal wage scale with an entirely newly designed production. Since theatrical costume companies at times replenish their rental stock through the purchase of an entire show no longer in the repertoire, designers may find costumes for their low budget opera projects, which form a stylistic unit, and to which new principal's costumes can be added in harmony with that style. In such events designers are able to create costumes for the principal performers that do justice not only to the many demands of a specific role, within the concept of the entire production, but also consider the figures and personalities of the individual interpreters of the part. Within reason it is even possible to cater to their likes and dislikes.

It has become fashionable to update opera plots to the present day. The reasons given for these procedures are in my estimation rationalizations without any basis in point. Stage-directors and designers for operas should instead be willing to emulate opera musicians who are satisfied to reinterpret the scores ever anew. As exponents of our own time we cannot fail to look and listen to the old masterpieces on our own terms and interpret them accordingly. I am not a priori against a shift of the time and place of a given opera, but the pros and cons must be weighed very carefully and seriously, not frivolously as is most often the case. In the ensuing chapters the reader will discover how I deal with these matters.

Very early in my career as a designer of opera costumes I concluded that the free-lance field did not suit me psychologically. I wanted a steady job and in that respect I have been fortunate. I was the staff costume designer for the New England Opera Theater (later the Goldovsky Grand Opera) during its entire existence, almost forty years. For twenty years I was head of the Opera Department of the Brooks Van Horn Costume Company and I was lucky to serve on the faculties of the Berkshire Music Center in Tanglewood, The Juilliard School, and the Curtis Institute of Music in Philadelphia. Because of these special circumstances I was able to observe operatic talents from their student days through their entire careers. Because all opera singers moonlight I had a chance to costume the beginners as well as those fully established and famous. In my professional relationship with these people I evidently managed to convey that I know my business and that I have no axe to grind. They accepted, that within the realm of the role's requirements I tried to make them look as good, and feel as comfortable, as possible.

I was fortunate also to costume not merely the standard repertoire, but world premieres and American premieres, among the latter masterworks of such disparate composers as Mozart and Benjamin Britten. I consider myself lucky also in being able to derive sufficient satisfaction in the knowledge of a job well done, without resorting to extremes in a desperate attempt to make audiences and reviewers at long last, 'sit up and take notice.' I do not consider that to be "The Costume Designer's Function."

CHAPTER *1*

VERDI'S

Illus. 1

Un Ballo in Maschera

"WILL THESE PEOPLE NEVER LEARN!" the censor may well have exclaimed, after reading the libretto of *Un Ballo in Maschera*. Indeed, Verdi and his librettist Somma could have figured out that if in 1851 the censor objected to having King Francis I of France depicted as an immoral and frivolous character, they would in 1858 be even less inclined to permit King Gustavus III of Sweden being killed on stage. As a matter of fact, Verdi and his librettist did anticipate some trouble on that score and toyed with the idea of changing the locale and the time of the story. It was the attack on the life of Napoleon III in the following year, however, that gave the censor a near heart attack, which resulted in almost line-by-line censorship of the opera's libretto.

One may ponder what induced the composer and his librettist to settle on Boston's alleged Governor, the Earl of Warwick (See

1

chapter-opening illustration, 1)* as a means of appeasing the censor. There existed indeed a person by the name of Robert Rich, who became Earl of Warwick in 1619, and who eventually headed the Commission of the New World Colonies. Assuming that he actually resided in Boston, that would have put the story in the 17th century, when masked balls in the Boston Opera House were few and far between, if indeed any existed. To Europeans, America had an aura of mystery even as late as the mid 19th century. 'Think of the possibilities!' a librettist might exclaim; 'there can be Indians, and Puritans, and Negroes! Madame Arvidson could be The Witch of Salem!' Yet to this listener the plot and the music of *Un Ballo* sound oddly un-American, and the historical inaccuracies of the Swedish setting are less bothersome than the American ones. True, Gustavus III was homosexual. He was also married and had a son who succeeded him to the throne.

Unlike Auber's score on the same subject, Verdi's omits entirely the reasons for the nobles' resentment against their king. He had abrogated some of their privileges and had made it plain that the pursuits of the Arts and the Theatre were of far greater importance to him. From the costumer's point of view it is interesting to observe that Gustavus had conceived a National Swedish costume (2, 3), which he naturally expected his subjects to wear. These costumes were not intended to be worn by the common people, who were not lacking in clothes that had a strong Swedish character. It was the aristocrats and courtiers whom he expected to forego the popular French fashions of the day in favor of his concepts. This did not sit well with these ladies and gentlemen, many of whom refused to accede to his wishes. Gustavus' costume ideas were not very original. In part they hark back to a somewhat earlier period, especially in the application of Stuart collars and puffed, slashed sleeves for the ladies and small shoulder loops for the men. There is a strong resemblance to the theatrical costumes worn at that time. Compare for instance Chodowieki's illustrations for Beaumarchais' *Figaro* (4). For costumers of the opera this situation is a godsend, for it enables them to demonstrate visually who are the King's adherents and who are his foes.

Ed. Note: Throughout this book you will find numbers in parentheses within the running text. These are designed to cross-refer you to related illustrations within a given chapter and to illustrate the points presented by the author. The first such cross-reference in a chapter usually, *but not always,* is to the chapter-opening illustration. Consequently, whenever given text within a chapter is related to the chapter-opening illustration, this is so indicated with a cross-reference in parenthesis referring the reader to the chapter-opening illustration and its illustration number.

Délicieuse créature!

TOP: Illus. 2; BOTTOM, LEFT: Illus. 3; BOTTOM, RIGHT: Illus. 4.

ACT I   SCENE 1

In the King's reception room, army officers, noblemen, delegates of the people, and the Counts Ribbing and Horn with their followers are present. The latter, usually referred to as 'the conspirators,' are dressed in somber-colored fashionable suits of the period: cutaway coats with matching knee breeches, slightly contrasting, but harmonizing vests, and jabots. Their own hair is fashionably styled in a queue. They all carry swords and have tricorn hats under the arm. In the 18th century any civilian of even the slightest rank (Mozart among them) carried a sword as a matter of course. The King's adherents were dressed in the National Costume (5). It consisted of a hip length, single-breasted tailored coat, often embellished with some braid. The sleeves were decorated with a row of loops at the shoulder. Sometimes the coat was of the 'cutaway' genre. Shoulder capes were frequently worn, as well as medium-sized brimmed hats, with some plumes at the side of the crown. An important part of the costume was a wide-waist sash, wrapped around twice and ending in a large bow of many loops, the short, hanging ends decorated with fringe. Knee breeches to match the coats were occasionally decorated with the same braid that trimmed the coats, but they did not vary in cut from those fashionable at the time. The choice of colors and of fabrics depended on the taste of the wearer and on the occasion of the costume's use. White powdered queue wigs accompanied these suits.

The military personnel in attendance wore the same style of uniforms (6) that were worn all over Europe at that time. The only Swedish touch was the choice of color, which was a medium blue with tan trim. Black over-the-knee boots were the usual foot wear, while the white wigs were covered by white-edged black tricorns with a military decoration at the side.

Since the King is receiving petitions it is to be expected that there are some humble folks in the crowd to deliver these. There is a large selection of Swedish folk costume (7) to choose from, which nevertheless adhered in some respects to the fashions of the time, especially in the popularity of laced bodices for women and of knee breeches for men. However, these are poor people who have come to petition and the clothes must bear out their status in the choice of colors and fabrics.

As is to be expected, the King also wears the National Costume

TOP, LEFT: Illus. 5; TOP, RIGHT: Illus. 6; BOTTOM: Illus. 7.

he has devised, but for its color he selected the blue of his officer's uniforms. He is the only civilian in that color. He too wears a white-powdered wig. Oscar is dressed in a Page's version of the King's invention, which varies from the others only in being of a very light blue and sporting a lace collar and cuffs. His hat has a small slashed brim, like the shoulder loops. It has a small puffed crown, and short plumes at the side.

Ankerstroem also wears the National Costume in a warm sympathetic shade. Over-the-knee boots and a shoulder cape will set him apart from the others.

The Chief Magistrate is not officiating on this occasion, and therefore a three-piece black suit with the judicial white tabs at the chin as the only means of identification, would suffice for him. His argument would carry more weight however (and be theatrically more effective) if he donned his ample black judicial robes (8) and wore the white judge's wig to top off his imposing appearance.

No palace can function without lackies and Gustavus' are naturally attired in a lackey version of the National Costume.

ACT I   SCENE 2

The Swedish painter Pehr Hillestroem has provided us with much information about 18th-century Swedish dress of working people as well as of the aristocracy (9), which comes in good stead for the scene in the fortune teller's hut. It is important to make it noticeable that the women and children who open this scene are in the daily folk costumes of the Uppland region wherein Stockholm lies, while the men who enter subsequently are in disguise. These disguises consist of men's everyday working clothes, which to officers and courtiers of that period would function as disguises. Through the selection of awkwardly matched components for these costumes this may subtly come across to the audience. The effect can be reinforced if the performers act somewhat ill at ease in their attire and evince some amusement at each other's looks. A student of Swedish folk costume will not fail to observe the popularity of knitted red stocking caps for men (10). All the disguised men in this scene should wear such stocking caps in a variety of colors, while the single bright red one remains reserved for Oscar. Alas, the Swedish sailor's costume of that

TOP: Illus. 8; BOTTOM: Illus. 9.

period also includes such a stocking cap, in beige to be sure to match his short, double-breasted jacket and full-knee breeches (11). The jacket is worn open over a striped, knitted shirt. If that shirt were striped in white and blue and the stocking cap matched it, the problem would be solved.

The King's fisherman's disguise should have some leather elements in it of the 'souwester' type including ample thigh-high black boots and a short leather jacket (12). He wears this over a dark-knitted shirt. His breeches are also dark and made of a rough home-spun fabric. He carries a large fishnet over his shoulder. Period wigs were not part of such working men's appearance.

Unlike any of the other women in this scene, Madame Arvidson is dressed entirely in black. Her costume is of a Puritan severity (12). Yet it must also convey a sense of mystery and sensuousness, which can be achieved through a sheer black overlay of the costume, and a shawl of mixed black, grey, and purple sheers, which also partly covers her rather austere hairdo.

Amelia's servant wears a dark woolen suit of the period, though a little old fashioned in cut. A simple black tricorn hat covers his hair which is pulled back in a queue. His hose are dark.

Amelia makes five appearances in the opera. It is curious to observe that in three of those she is hiding her identity. For her secret visit to Madame Arvidson she wears a hooded cloak of a somber color. The Stuart collar, which is part of Gustavus' lady's costume, protrudes at the neck and prevents the hood from functioning as a head cover. Instead Amelia conceals her face behind a veil which covers her coiffure and face (13). Evidently the veil is heavy enough to hide Amelia's features, but not so heavy that her voice is inaudible through it. The Stuart collar should be visible in all her appearances, becoming, so to speak her 'trademark.'

ACT II

In the gallows scene Amelia might repeat her costume from the previous act, but being a lady of some substance she most likely chose another dark-hued cape, this time trimmed with fur (14). The veil which covers her face is for the purpose of security pinned to her coiffure, or maybe even to a hat. In order to protect her husband from

TOP, LEFT: Illus. 10; TOP, RIGHT: Illus. 11; BOTTOM, LEFT: Illus. 12;
BOTTOM, RIGHT: Illus. 13.

Horn and Ribbing's threatened assault Amelia reveals her identity by removing the hatpin, which causes the veil to drop and thus bare her features.

Although it is unlikely that the King would have ventured to such a location without a cape, the plot does not permit it, for there would have been no reason then for Ankerstroem to give his cape to the King. Instead Gustavus will wear over his indoor costume a long outdoor coat, quite likely fur trimmed (15). Ankerstroem had put on a cape in order to be able to move undetected among the conspirators. Evidently no conspirator would be found without one.

ACT III   SCENE 1

Amelia and Ankerstroem enter the latter's study in their house, dressed in the same clothes they wore in the previous Scene. Having given his cape to the King, Ankerstroem reveals the National Swedish costume, which he wore underneath. When Amelia returns with Oscar, we see her for the first time not in disguise, but wearing a becoming daytime dress of the period,with modest paniers and the Stuart collar and slashed and puffed sleeves that were part of the lady's National costume (16). Oscar is again in his page boy's costume and Ribbing and Horn also repeat their Act I, Scene 1 attire.

ACT III   SCENE 2

Before attending the Ball, the King wears a variation of the suits he has worn before, or he might be in a dressing gown. He is the eternal optimist and nothing in his appearance should give the slightest hint of any concern in connection with the threats and warnings he has received.

Oscar is already dressed for the Ball and a Harlequin's costume (17) seems ideal for him. It suits his character as well as the music he will sing later on in this scene.

Masked balls were a popular form of entertainment in the 18th century. Contemporary illustrations of such events reveal that a great deal of freedom reigned in the choice of what to wear to such festivities. Those who did not wish to put on anything out of the

TOP, LEFT: Illus. 14; TOP, RIGHT: Illus. 15; BOTTOM, LEFT: Illus. 16;
BOTTOM, RIGHT: Illus. 17.

ordinary could restrict their participation to the wearing of a mask (18). To others the easy way out consisted in wrapping themselves in a 'Domino' (19). Dominos were initially large hoods attached to shouldercapes, worn by monks. For masquerade purposes they developed into wide-sleeved, ample, floor-length hooded robes. They were frequently half black and half white, but not necessarily so. They could be of any color. The costumes of the *commedia dell'arte* comedies, always worn with masks, were a frequent source of inspiration for masquerade purposes. The exotic attraction of the clothes of faraway lands never failed to exert its influence for such events. Turks, with huge turbans, Chinese, Indians, they all would find their way to *Un Ballo in Maschera*. The masks worn on such occasions also varied widely from simple black half masks, to the most extravagantly stylized animal faces, with large beaks.

After quite a bit of prodding Oscar reveals that the King will wear a black domino with pink ribbons, while the conspirators wear blue dominos with red scarves. That implies, of course, that no one else on stage must wear these colors.

The only mention of Amelia's costume (20) states that she wears a white robe, symbolizing her innocence no doubt. In her emotional turmoil, she may have spent little time considering what to wear to the ball, except that once again she did not want to be recognized. If symbolize we must, a reversal of the King's colors seems appropriate, hence: a domino of pink brocade and a simple black half mask, will be the choice. The Stuart collar, this time richly decorated will also be in evidence, while a fan will aid her in disguising her voice. Amelia should by no means be the only one to avail herself of this popular accessory.

TOP: Illus. 18; BOTTOM: Illus. 19.

Illus. 20.

CHAPTER 2

PUCCINI'S

Madama Butterfly

Illus. 21

*C*AST LISTS OF THE OPERA'S scores, libretti, or programs frequently record its time of action as: The Present. This may be a left over from the original production, for the events as they unfold in the plot would certainly no longer occur in our time. The opera had its disastrous premiere in 1904, and the time of action should be no later than: Turn Of The Century.

What can be said about the costumes of *Madama Butterfly*? A Gertrude Stein devotee might reflect that after all "A Kimono is a Kimono is a Kimono." Further investigation will reveal that this is a gross generalization. A multitude of variations exists, which the costumer must exploit for the sake of the identification of the various characters, the occasion of their use, and the prevailing mood. Space does not permit a discussion of all these variations, but this volume's bibliography will reveal some sources where this information can be found.

To the Japanese the nape of a woman's neck has a sensual attraction. The kimonos of unmarried women are therefore always worn with its collar pushed down in the back, thus exposing that part of her anatomy. (See Chapter-opening photo, 21) It is a characteristic that has escaped virtually all non-Japanese interpreters of the opera's title role. True, to position the kimono in that fashion, and to prevent it from sliding back, takes some doing. In Japanese department stores a gadget can be purchased especially constructed for that purpose. A tape is attached inside the middle-back collar's edge of the under-kimono. From there it descends as far as the waistline where it is joined to a cross tape which ties around the waist, thereby holding matters firmly in place. The fact that such a contraption is being sold in modern Japan indicates the importance that is still attached to this detail. Although Western dress now prevails in Japan, kimonos and the equivalent Japanese male attire are still worn for special occasions, religious and otherwise, and can be observed sporadically in daily wear among older people. At a recent performance at the Metropolitan Opera House (not of *Madama Butterfly*) a large number of Japanese happened to be in the audience. Almost all the ladies among them wore kimonos.

* * * *

Male characters in order of appearance: Pinkerton

Lieutenant B. F. Pinkerton wears the white summer uniform of a lieutenant in the U.S. Navy (22). Its single-breasted coat is closed with gold metal buttons. Black shoulder-boards have two gold stripes at the outer edge and one gold star, denoting his rank. The visor cap has a white crown with the gold embroidered navy emblem in the middle front, and a shiny black visor. His shoes are black. Although it is again summer when Pinkerton returns three years later, it is theatrically valid that he now wear the more subdued navy blue winter uniform (23), because of the different circumstances and the prevailing somber mood.

SHARPLESS

The American General Consul in Nagasaki would naturally be dressed in a fairly formal summer daytime suit of the period. It

LEFT: Illus. 22; RIGHT: Illus. 23.

does not seem likely that he would wear Japanese clogs, as is mentioned in the play. Because he does not share Pinkerton's light-hearted attitude, and keeps warning him of its impropriety, the color of his suit should be rather subdued. He is quite apt to carry a straw Stetson hat (24). Not to give him a change of costume for his second appearance is a serious error, which is nevertheless frequently perpetrated. Not only is it unlikely that he would wear the identical suit again three years later, the occasion and the mood now demand a much more formal and dignified appearance (25). A dark grey, three-piece cutaway suit is suggested instead, with a wing collar and Ascot tie, a matching Homburg hat, and spats.

GORO

Goro, the marriage broker, wears partially Western clothes, consisting of a black bowler hat and a plaid tweed jacket, combined with Japanese pants (hakama) and clogs (26). This will be his costume throughout the opera's three acts. It is, so to speak, his uniform, never to be changed.

MALE SERVANTS

Upon Suzuki's first appearance in the opera's opening scene, she enters with two men who are introduced to Pinkerton as a 'Cook' and a 'Servant.' Later on in the proceedings a third male servant is mentioned. Their costumes are of a modest nature, consisting of a male kimono-like top, tucked into hakama trousers, joined by an equally modest sash (27). The middle section of their heads is shaven bald (28).

Prince Yamadori is accompanied by two servants who carry flowers. Since he is a wealthy man, his servants are accordingly somewhat more ostentatiously dressed, as far as the quality of the fabric and the colors of their garments is concerned. They also wear an additional short outergarment, the 'haori.'

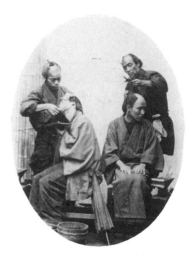

TOP, LEFT; Illus. 24; TOP, RIGHT: Illus. 25; BOTTOM, LEFT: Illus. 26; BOTTOM, RIGHT: Illus. 27 and 28.

MALE RELATIVES

The only male relatives who are identified in the score are an uncle Yakuside, who likes wine, and a little boy, who likes sweets. All the others are anonymous. They wear variations of the male Japanese everyday costume: the male version of the kimono, the 'hakama' (pants), the 'haori' (short overgarment) or the 'happi' (short outdoor coat) (29). Printed cotton is most often used for these garments, whose decorations are carefully planned. The cone-shaped straw hats (30) are popular as protection against the sun, but the omission of any head gear is a frequent occurrence.

The little boy wears a printed cotton kimono to suit his size. A page boy hairstyle is suitable for him.

COMMISSIONER AND REGISTRAR

From the Kabuki stage costumes one may borrow the large shoulder-winged jumpers called 'kataginu,' (31) which added to the usual man's costume lend it an air of officialdom. The partly bald wig is suitable for them as well.

BONZE

The Bonze, Cio Cio San's uncle, wears the austere attire of a Japanese priest consisting of a black robe under the voluminous seven-eighth length over-robe with its gigantic kimono sleeves, and tight white under-sleeves (32). The headdress consists of a small black pillbox to which a tall black loop is added in the middle back. The hat is tied under the chin. A sinister brownish yellow seems a good color for the Bonze's over-robe, which is without ornamentation.

PRINCE YAMADORI

Prince Yamadori became a rich man while he resided in New York. It is therefore entirely plausible that he should wear Western men's clothes (33). As the wooing bridegroom-to-be, a black cutaway

TOP, LEFT: Illus. 29; TOP, RIGHT: Illus. 30; BOTTOM, LEFT: Illus. 31;
BOTTOM, RIGHT: Illus. 32.

coat, grey-and-black striped pants, a grey double-breasted vest, an Ascot tie and a black top hat would make him look truly ridiculous. An argument against this style of costume is also acceptable. In that case, ostentatiously rich Japanese attire is in order.

TROUBLE

To costume a two-year, and-three-month-old child is no problem. To be able to cast a child of that age is a problem indeed, for Trouble must be entirely passive during his presence on stage, which is hardly standard behavior for such an infant, unless it has been tranquilized. As a result children that are quite a bit older often take the role, which hardly adds to the credibility. Finding an older child who is unusually tiny for his age is probably the best solution. It might just as well be a girl, so long as it has blond hair and blue eyes. Even the latter will hardly be noticeable across the footlights. Trouble is seen for the first time upon Sharpless' Second Act visit, when his mother unexpectedly produces him, and the child wears whatever he happened to have on at the moment, most likely a tiny light blue kimono (34), if blue for boys and pink for girls is also a Japanese custom.

When Suzuki dresses him before the vigil, it is in anticipation of his father's arrival, therefore a tiny white sailor suit (35), with a blue sailor collar and even a sailor's cap will be in order. That will also harmonize with the American flag Cio Cio San will put in his hand later on.

* * * *

Female characters in order of appearance: Suzuki

Suzuki is the first female character to appear on the scene, and she proves to be a very important one. If Cio Cio San lives in an ever optimistic never-never land, Suzuki is a realist, who constantly apprises her mistress of the facts of life. The latter does not take that too well and threatens to kill her servant on various occasions. Yet there is no doubt of the bond of affection between the two.

Servants' kimonos differed from their mistresses in the quality of

TOP: Illus. 33; BOTTOM, LEFT: Illus. 34; BOTTOM, RIGHT; Illus. 35.

the fabric and the mode of decoration (36). Cotton instead of silk in case of the former, printed rather than painted or embroidered concerning the latter. The length of the kimono's sleeves and the greater simplicity of the obi and its bow, also played a part. Occasionally an apron was worn.

Speaking of kimonos, which incidentally overlap in front from left to right, it is important to observe that they are not shortened or lengthened as an adjustment to the height of the wearer by 'taking up,' or 'letting down' the hem, which is never touched. Instead a fold is made in the fabric at the waist region, to establish the proper length. This almost creates the effect of a two-piece garment. The obi helps in preventing the fold from unfolding, but for stage purposes there are more secure ways, like pinning or sewing to control the fold.

After three years Suzuki will no longer wear the same kimono she had on in Act I, although in character and color it will be similar (37). Suzuki's wig is a simplified version of her mistress' and devoid of hair ornaments.

CIO CIO SAN

After she was heard singing off-stage, Cio Cio San enters dressed in her wedding kimono (38), and carrying a parasol. The kimono may be white, with colored decorations, but white is not obligatory. This may prove to be a blessing in case the singer's vital statistics leave something to be desired. Yet, even when the kimono is white, the decorations can be applied in ways that will create a slenderizing effect. Whatever the kimono's color, the nape of the neck is still exposed. The bridal headgear is not everybody's favorite. Yet, it is so typical that one should be very loathe to omit it. The wedding obi with its thick multi-looped bow, might be modified to soften a somewhat hump-backed effect it creates in Western eyes. When one observes pictures of the hairdos of various Cio Cio San interpreters through the ages, the variety, even including bangs, is astounding, although not surprising. The Japanese woman's hairdo of the past is very typical and bears no fooling around with. Yet it also came in many variations (39a,b; 40a,b), and the one most flattering to a specific performer can be found. Of all the costume items of this opera, the wigs must be entrusted to professional hands. Their clean-cut sculptured contours

TOP, LEFT: Illus. 36; TOP, RIGHT; Illus. 37; BOTTOM: Illus. 38.

and the clearly defined point in the middle front, bear no modification. This applies to all the female Japanese characters in the opera, although age and character naturally play a part.

Cio Cio San's make-up is close enough to the realm of costuming to warrant some mention here. In the Oriental's face the upper eyelid is not visible. This fact seems to bother modern Japanese ladies enough to have it surgically "corrected." For theatrical purposes the upper eyelid can simply be drawn on top of the overhanging flesh, if the face is an Oriental one. On a Western face the omission of any eye shadow will suffice. An effort must also be made to give the eyes a slanted look. Geishas made their faces up white, and so must Cio Cio San and her girl friends. Hardly any rouge was applied and the lips are rose-bud shaped. After her 'marriage' Cio Cio San can forego the white make-up. A good Oriental skin color must now be applied for her instead and, in varying shades, for all the other Japanese members of the cast.

Before retiring to the bridal chamber, Cio Cio San exchanges the wedding kimono for an all white bridal negligee of a soft silk (41). It is also cut along kimono lines, and when worn open, without an obi, over an under-kimono of a darker hue, this can be flattering to the figure. After the removal of the wedding headgear, the hair remains dressed. From a variety of flattering, and at times elaborate hair ornaments, including flowers, those most appropriate for this particular bride must be selected. One might now expect to see the hair loose, but this is not so. Many pictures exist of Japanese women in repose, with the hair still dressed (42).

After the three years' interval, some producers like to dress Cio Cio San in Western dress, thereby indicating her desire to please her American husband, and to emphasize her status as Mrs. B. F. Pinkerton. In matters of dress Japanese women used to be extremely conservative, Cio Cio San no less so. She may change her religion because she believes she may become an American, but she would not change her mode of dressing. From a theatrical point of view such a change would also steal Kate Pinkerton's thunder. She must remain the only woman in the cast in Western dress.

After the passing of three years Cio Cio San wears a pleasing, young married woman's kimono, which covers the nape of the neck. In appearance it will bear witness to the subdued mood and circumstances of the occasion. Her hair is also modestly but flatteringly decorated. Upon learning of Pinkerton's return, she changes into her

**TOP, LEFT: Illus. 39a,b; TOP, RIGHT: Illus. 40a,b; BOTTOM, LEFT:
Illus. 41; BOTTOM, RIGHT: Illus. 42.**

wedding kimono, but omits the wedding headdress. When she appears from behind the screen with the veil around her neck, her hair is sometimes shown hanging loose down her back, requiring of course a change of wig. This may be theatrically effective although there is no mention of it in the score.

THE GIRLFRIENDS

The temptation to dress the chorus of Cio Cio San's girlfriends identically must be resisted. *Madama Butterfly* is not a musical comedy and the girlfriends do not constitute a chorus line. Yet the colors and design of their kimonos (43a) must be closely coordinated, as well as their obis, parasols, and hairdos. They, as well as all the other women in the cast except Suzuki, carry fans (43b) which may be stuck in the obis when not in use.

THE FEMALE RELATIVES

Cio Cio San's mother, aunt, and cousin are the only characters singled out from the chorus of female relatives. According to their ages and character they can wear varying kimonos, obis, and wigs (44, 45a, 45b). In that respect one may apply some Western standards regarding the colors: the older the darker, as well as in the way the obis are draped; longer ends hanging down for the older ladies, shorter obi ends for the younger generation. It goes without saying that for theatrical purposes the obis, and especially their bows, can be pre-tied. The obis can then be closed through the use of hooks and eyes. Several rows of hooks will make the waist size adjustable. The women's coiffures and hair ornaments also respond to their ages and character. A smattering of parasols is in order for them as well, and they must all carry fans.

KATE PINKERTON

An elegant, light-colored summer-afternoon gown of the turn of the century is appropriate for Kate (46). Since her vocal part is

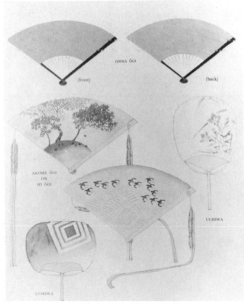

TOP, LEFT: Illus. 43a; BOTTOM, RIGHT: Illus. 43b.

minimal in the opera's final version, she may as well be cast for her good looks and handsome figure. A large brimmed hat, a pocketbook, gloves, and a parasol (Western style), are all harmonious parts of her ensemble.

JAPANESE FOOTWEAR

One aspect of Japanese costume that may cause a conflict is the footwear (see 47). Inside the house Japanese wore only tabis, which are socks with a separate space for the big toe. Sandals or clogs are worn only out of doors. They are left outside, lined up in front of the house before entering. It is a curious sight to behold and to this native-born Hollander reminiscent of Dutch peasants, whose wooden shoes can also be observed lined-up outside, in front of the farm.

In the opera a compromise has to be reached, since in the first act almost everybody enters from outside, and there is neither time nor place to dispose of the footwear. If the sandals match in color those of the tabis no one will be the wiser. In deference to this custom Westerners also remove their shoes upon entering a Japanese home. It is suggested that Kate Pinkerton be excused on this occasion from following that practice.

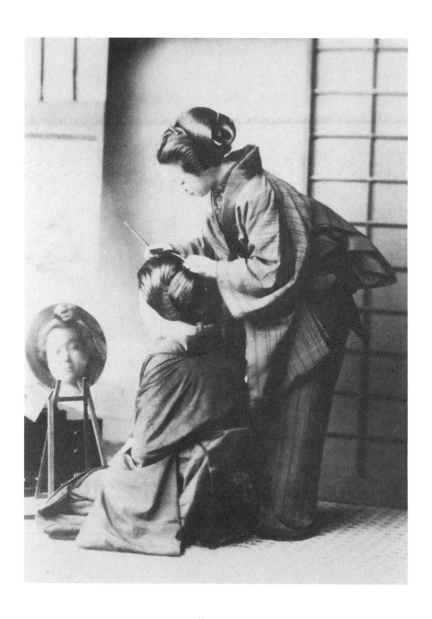

Illus. 44.

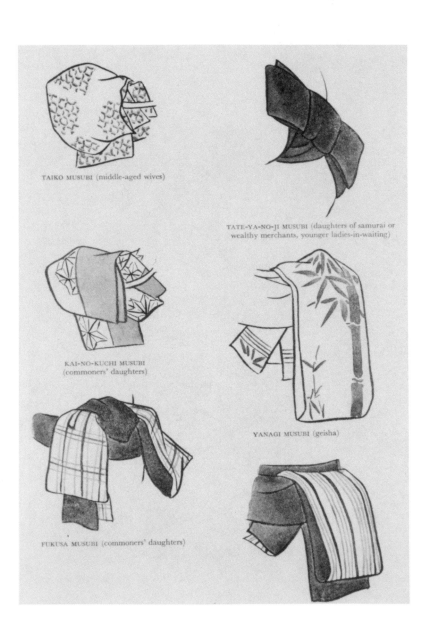

TAIKO MUSUBI (middle-aged wives)

TATE-YA-NO-JI MUSUBI (daughters of samurai or wealthy merchants, younger ladies-in-waiting)

KAI-NO-KUCHI MUSUBI (commoners' daughters)

YANAGI MUSUBI (geisha)

FUKUSA MUSUBI (commoners' daughters)

Illus. 45a.

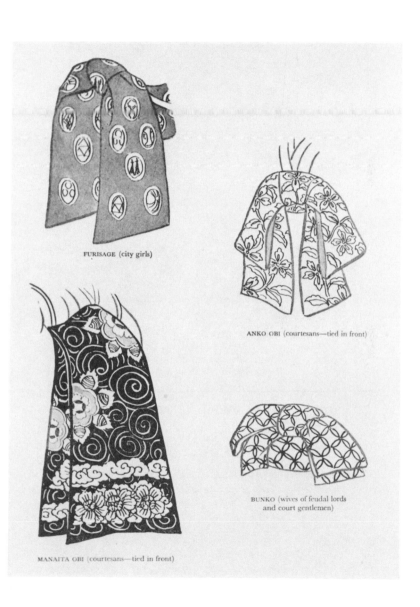

FURISAGE (city girls)

ANKO OBI (courtesans—tied in front)

MANAITA OBI (courtesans—tied in front)

BUNKO (wives of feudal lords and court gentlemen)

Illus. 45b.

Illus. 46.

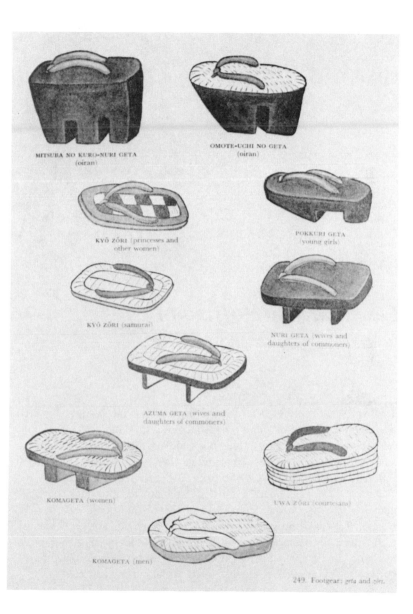

MITSUBA NO KURO-NURI GETA
(oiran)

OMOTE-UCHI NO GETA
(oiran)

KYŌ ZŌRI (princesses and
other women)

POKKURI GETA
(young girls)

KYŌ ZŌRI (samurai)

NURI GETA (wives and
daughters of commoners)

AZUMA GETA (wives and
daughters of commoners)

KOMAGETA (women)

UWA ZŌRI (courtesans)

KOMAGETA (men)

249. Footgear: geta and zōri.

Illus. 47.

CHAPTER 3

OFFENBACH'S

Illus. 48

Les Contes d'Hoffmann

*T*HE PLAY BY BARBIER AND CARRÉ from which the authors distilled the libretto for *Les Contes d'Hoffmann* was called "Les Contes Fantastiques d'Hoffmann." The omission of 'Fantastique' is significant. Although it was most likely done merely to shorten, and hence improve the opera's title, Offenbach also proceeded to exclude the 'fantastic' from the opera's music. Attempts to introduce fantastic elements into the visual realization of the opera should be resisted, because they have proven detrimental to the music. The film version of the opera, in which there was 'fantastique' aplenty has experienced no clamor for reruns, while the opera manages to retain its place in the repertoire without such excursions into visual extravagance.

No opera has been produced in more different versions than *Hoffmann,* owing to the fact that the composer did not live to supervise the production of his opera, which had to be left to others, notably Guiraud (known to us primarily for his *Carmen* recitatives).

36

Furthermore, until very recently much additional music for the opera, from the composer's pen has been discovered, which he might, or might not have incorporated in the opera's final version. Luckily none of these discoveries have altered the opera's plot or its characters, nor the way they should be costumed. Some other features of the opera require clarification, however. Of these the time element is the most important one. E. T. A. Hoffmann, the opera's leading man, does not appear as a character in any of the many stories he wrote, nor does he indicate in any of his many 'tales' when they are supposed to have occurred. Hoffmann lived from 1776 till 1822, wherefore we may assume that the stories in the opera took place at various times during the author's life from age 16 onward. (He was no doubt a precocious lover.)

The chronology of the stories is not entirely clear. Nicklausse names them at one point in the following order: Olympia, Antonia, Giulietta. On the stage, however, the Antonia scene is usually performed as Act III.

In what quick succession the different affairs occurred is not known either. It all depends how severe was Hoffmann's obsession that as a lover he was doomed, and how often he felt the need to prove this to himself. To this writer the solution to these speculations is that each story has its own musical atmosphere. They also suggest an appropriate historical period within the span of Hoffmann's life for each story. Accordingly, the Prologue and Epilogue occur towards the end of the author's brief life, around 1822. The fashions of 1820 seem especially suitable for the Olympia story (Chapter-opening illustration, 48). Giulietta's tale breathes a strong 'Empire' feeling (49), while the domestic atmosphere of Antonia's story suggests the Biedermeier time, around 1830 (50). True, that is about eight years after Hoffmann's death, but a poet of his nature was bound to have had a posthumous affair.

PROLOGUE

The students who gather at Luther's tavern are of the college or university level. Before World War I, German students of that kind wore, what was for all practical purposes, a military uniform (51). It consisted of a single-breasted, hip-length uniform coat, vertically braided from chest to waist. The color of the coat depended on the

Illus. 49.

TOP: Illus. 50; BOTTOM: Illus. 51.

university they attended. White ankle tights went in to knee-high black boots. Small pillbox-type hats covered part of the heads, which were frequently shaven bald. White gauntlets were de rigueur, as well as wide order sashes. For a price students could get their faces scarred, to suggest participation in duels.

It is proposed that the opera's four villains: Lindorf, Coppelius, Dappertutto and Dr. Miracle, wear similar, but not identical, costumes which make them easily identifiable. As luck will have it, a popular male outer garment of that period lends itself especially well for that purpose. It is the double-, triple- or even quadruply-caped, greatcoat or Carrick (52). Through their volume and length they can make an appropriately ominous impression, and yet offer plenty of opportunity for individuality. Naturally, no one else in the cast must wear such a garment. In the ensuing chapters an alternate mode of costuming for some of these gentlemen is suggested as well.

According to Councillor Lindorf's description of himself, he is old and ugly (53). Under these circumstances it would be difficult for him to compete with younger rivals for the favors of Stella, the Italian diva, who at this moment is all the rage with Nuremberg opera audiences. Lindorf, on the other hand, claims to have 'satanic wit' and . . . he is rich! He wears an almost ankle-length, dark grey Carrick with a triple cape, of which the top one is of fur, as is the coat's high, turn-over collar. A matching beaver top hat, gloves, and a cane complete his costume. To wear a hat inside such a locale was the habit then for men and women customers.

Andres is Stella's servant, who comes to deliver a letter from her to Hoffmann. Lindorf buys the letter from him, and Andres proves that he cannot be bought for a farthing. One would expect a diva of Stella's standing to dress her servants in style. Andres wears a simple lackey suit with matching coat and breeches, a contrasting vest without braid, and with metal buttons. A cotton jabot and cuff ruffles, cloth leggings, black shoes, no powdered wig, and a small black bicorn will do nicely for him.

A visitor to Bavaria will find evidence of the persistent popularity of Tyrolian costume elements. In the evening ladies can on occasion be observed wearing elegant 'dirndls' with aprons and laced bodices on festive occasions, while on men Tyrolian hats, jackets, and leder-hosen are not infrequently seen. This kind of dress seems especially suited for Luther, the tavern owner (54), and his waiters. The latter can wear identical shirts under the typical embroidered Tyrolian suspend-

TOP, LEFT: Illus. 52; BOTTOM, RIGHT: Illus. 53.

ers. Their lederhosen are partly hidden by half aprons. A desire for uniformity is an important German trait.

Hoffmann's friends—Nathaniel, Hermann and Wilhelm—are occasionally dressed in uniform. This would imply that they are also students, which is incorrect. They may be younger than Hoffmann, but they are beyond the 'student' age. They wear various cloth frock coats of the period, with pants of a lighter shade and contrasting, but harmonizing vests, fashionable neckwear and top hats of various shapes and sizes, but nothing so formidable as Lindorf's (55).

Hoffmann himself is at a pretty 'down' stage of his life. He has thrown in the towel as far as his amorous conquests are concerned, and all he wants to do now is smoke, and above all: drown his sorrow in drink! Such a mood naturally reflects in his costume, which is a pretty somber frock suit of the period. He is never addressed, or referred to other than 'Poet,' which makes it necessary to make him look like a poet, regardless of his mood. An open-neck shirt without cravat is essential. A beret too will give him an artistic touch (56). If that is not sufficient he may replace his velvet frock coat with a shouldercape, worn over one shoulder, with the end of the other side thrown over that shoulder. That never misses to get the 'artist' message across.

Nicklausse is Hoffmann's friend, protector and eventually also his Muse. This change of gender is not so surprising, considering that the role is cast for a mezzo-soprano. Even as a friend Nicklausse displays some mother-hen instincts. When entering from outside he wears a long, tiered cape, over a tailsuit of the period, with boots and one of those visor caps that were fashionable then (57). It is suggested that he be the only one to wear such headgear. It is his trademark. Depending on the situation he may have removed the cape, once inside.

ACT I—OLYMPIA

Spalanzani is evidently a rich, eccentric, dilettante scientist and inventor, whose hobby it is to produce life-size and life-like dolls. Until the arrival of his guests he is wearing 'working clothes.' In 1820 eccentric old people frequently dressed 'ancien regime.' Therefore, Spalanzani can be expected to wear knee breeches, and a brocaded vest over a shirt with a lace jabot and lace cuff ruffles. A stylized wig, possibly with a high pompadour would go with that, as well as

TOP, LEFT: Illus. 54; BOTTOM, RIGHT: Illus. 55.

Illus. 56.

Illus. 57.

colored hose and buckled shoes (58). For laboratory purposes he may wear a bib-work apron. The latter he removes when his guests arrive and replaces it with a velvet cutaway coat. The colors of all parts of his costume may be vivid, and contrasting. He is somewhat of a caricature.

When Hoffmann upon his arrival apologizes for being early, Spalanzani refers to him as 'my student.' Whatever science he teaches Hoffmann, access to his workroom-laboratory was evidently not included, or there could be no 'Olympia Scene.' (59) Since the time of this scene must be evening, when supper is being served, Hoffmann wears a velvet frockcoat, with a dressy harmonizing vest and light pants, and naturally his trademarks—the open-neck shirt and beret. In this scene there is less emphasis on the 'poet' aspect of his personality, and hence no need to replace the frockcoat with an artistic cape.

Cochenille, Spalanzani's stuttering servant (60), is dressed in a subdued lackey's uniform, of which the individual parts may be ill-matched to emphasize his stutter. His own balding hair is tied in back with a ribbon.

Coppelius, the mad-scientist-crook, must have a lot of pockets in his shaggy, skimpy, very dark Carrick, with a single-shoulder cape (61). From these pockets he produces all the colored eye glasses. One of these he sells to Hoffmann, which causes the poet to believe that Olympia is a real 'living doll.'

Nicklausse does not require his cape in this act. So little of his tail suit was seen in the Prologue, that he can wear it again in this act with impunity.

Since it has been established that this is an evening event, the guests (see 59, 63), evidently a rich crowd, are in evening attire of the period, with stoles and shawls for the ladies and top hats for the gentlemen.

Olympia is what in the domain of dolls is called a 'Fashion Doll,' in proportions and dress entirely a human replica, and in this case in size as well, which is less common. She wears a white, or off-white young woman's ball gown of the period (62, 63). A certain stiffness of the fabric is appropriate. The same applies to trimmings, like bows and ribbons. Her dress has a high neck, or the décolleté has been filled in with a matching sheer fabric, which also forms a shirred ruffle around her neck, and covers her arms. The less real flesh is shown the better. The ringlets of her fashionable hairdo are also stiff, as is the bow in her hair. Ruffled pantalettes, showing below the hem of her dress are

TOP: Illus. 58; BOTTOM: Illus. 59.

Illus. 60.

Illus. 61.

also helpful. She wears matching flat-heeled shoes. Whether any of the mechanism of the doll should be visible, like the screw to rewind it, is a matter of taste. It never fails to get a reaction from the audience.

ACT II—GIULIETTA

The Empire period, with its atmosphere of stately elegance, is particularly suited for the Guilietta episode.

Nicklausse wears the same cape and visor cap, but the suit underneath it must harmonize with Giulietta's costume, when they join to sing the Barcarolle seated in a gondola. Because Nicklausse is not exactly Giulietta's friend, wiser heads may decide to costume another mezzo soprano in male Empire attire, to join Giulietta in gondola and song.

Giulietta is a courtesan, which means that she is a lady with brains and good taste, but questionable morals. She is kept by a rich old man, in this case Dappertutto, but also bestows her favors on some younger fellows like Schlemil, Hoffmann, and Pitichinaccio, who in their turn pay a rather stiff price for those favors. Giulietta wears an elegant, sheer-brocaded Empire gown with its puffed sleeves, lace collar, and an Empire-type draped turban, trimmed with an aigrette and jewelled pin (64). She wears plenty of jewelry. Later on in the scene she may add a typically Empire court-mantle to her gown and replace the turban with a tiara. Among the guests the ladies wear modified versions of Giulietta's dress, accessorized with long stoles or shawls, Empire bonnets and occasional parasols. Empire ladies' shoes had no heels. If that causes a problem, the height of the heel must be kept to a minimum.

The Empire period offers a choice of suitable attire to the gentlemen of the ensemble (see 49), because it was a time of transition as far as men's dress was concerned. Especially for formal occasions velvet tailcoats and knee breeches, with brocaded vests were still in vogue, while for everyday wear cloth tailcoats and frock coats were worn with lighter colored pants, or ankle-tights with boots. They all share some features, however—namely, knuckle-length tight sleeves with some fullness at the shoulder. They all had high, stand-up collars, which were frequently folded over. Some coats had lapels, others shawl-collars. Much the same was true for the vests, which were

Illus. 62.

Illus. 63.

Illus. 64.

always of a contrasting fabric, usually single-breasted and with two points at the bottom. They invariably had a stand-up collar. Neckwear was equally distinguished with chin-covering pointed collars under draped neckcloths or silk scarves. Although bicorns were still in favor, top hats were the accepted male headcover. Their shape and height of crowns, as well as brims varied endlessly, which offers much opportunity for characterization.

The addition of some Empire uniforms (65) among such a crowd always is a visually pleasing variation. No doubt this scene also includes servants in appropriate lackey costumes as well as gondoliers (66).

For Hoffmann another velvet frock coat is indicated for this scene in addition to his 'poet's trademarks,' the open-neck collar and beret.

The choice of the Yiddish word 'schlemil' as the name for Giulietta's lover Peter is exactly right for this hapless sap who forfeited his shadow for the sake of her favors. Although this loss of shadow is symbolic, it would be nice to be able to make it somehow apparent in his appearance. Alas, such a feat is almost impossible to accomplish on the stage. Anyone who has ever been involved with a production of Richard Strauss' *Die Frau ohne Schatten* can attest to that. This writer would like to suggest that Schlemil (67) wear a dark leotard, on which a suit's shadow casting features are merely outlined in a lighter color. Incidentally, he also carries a sword. An attempt should be made as well to make Hoffmann's loss of his mirror image visual to the audience through the use of featureless make-up or a blank mask.

In Hoffmann's story, Dappertutto is described as wearing a red cape with metal buttons, which seems hardly appropriate for so sinister a character. A very dark, but heavily-braided Empire uniform (68), with matching ankle tights and black boots is more suitable for him. He wears this under a matching triple-tiered long cape with a high-folded collar. The cape might be lined in red. A large bicorn is also in order.

Pitichinaccio is one of those shadowy characters who appear, and disappear again, in a jiffy. At times he is referred to as a dwarf, which only makes sense if he is a very rich man. Nothing else could induce Giulietta to depart with such a creature. Accordingly he wears a brocaded 'ancien regime' costume, complete with a powdered wig and tricorn (69).

TOP: Illus. 65; MIDDLE: Illus. 66; BOTTOM: Illus. 67.

ACT III—ANTONIA

The term 'Biedermeier' and domesticity are almost synonymous, which makes this period so suitable for the Antonia scene. Councillor Crespel (70), Antonia's father, is either just coming in from outside, or he is just on his way out. It is wise, therefore, to costume him suitably for either circumstance. A knee-length dark redingote with a velvet collar, pants of a lighter shade and a brocaded vest will accomplish that. He may have left his beaver top hat outside upon entering.

With his 'Poet's trademarks' Hoffmann now wears an 1830 version of his former costume, including that poetic velvet coat (71). Franz, the deaf servant is well suited in domestic servant's livery, but without a coat. With his shirt sleeves he wears a cloth vest with matching knee breeches, grey hose, and buckled shoes. He has a bald pate.

It is important to stress Antonia's frailty through her costumes. The 1830 period is suitable for that, provided the leg o' mutton sleeves are limp and the gown's fabric is either sheer or very soft. The petticoats should not be stiff and her hairdo must be soft as well (72). A long lace stole may be a helpful accessory. For her second appearance and death scene, a soft, sheer negligee will create the proper feeling.

Dr. Miracle appears and disappears out of nowhere it seems. Although this is a problem to be solved mostly through 'stage magic,' it helps if his costume is dark enough (73) to make him unnoticeable in the stage's dark recesses, when the light is not on him. Tight black pants, a black tailcoat with sharp points at the tail, front, collar and lapels, plus a black vest with equally pointed bottom ends, will help to characterize him. His collar and black cravat should be pointed as well. Slick red hair with a satanic forelock is also called for. He requires a black doctor's bag in which to carry his magic paraphernalia.

The portrait of Antonia's mother should not represent an old lady, but rather a prima donna in her prime, in a dramatic dark décolleté gown (74). It is the typical dress in which a diva would have her portrait painted.

TOP, LEFT: Illus. 68; TOP, RIGHT: Illus. 69; BOTTOM: Illus. 70.

Illus. 71.

Illus. 72; BOTTOM: Illus. 73.

EPILOGUE

All the characters who appeared in the Prologue repeat their costumes in this act.

Stella, the Italian prima donna appears briefly in an elegant evening cape, extravagant hairdo and much jewelry (75). If the cape is not closed, it will reveal underneath an evening gown of equal splendor.

Nicklausse wears his cape now entirely closed (76), for he is underdressed as the Muse, who wears a classical flowing garment, possibly with a wreath of laurel leaves in her hair (77). Through the mere removal of his cape and boots, this transformation should not prove too taxing.

Illus. 74.

Illus. 75.

TOP: Illus. 76; BOTTOM: Illus. 77.

CHAPTER *4*

MOZART'S

Die Entführung aus dem Serail

*T*HROUGHOUT THE HISTORY of opera, librettists, composers, as well as audiences, have been fascinated by exotic alien cultures. From Rameau's *Les Indes Galantes,* via Rossini's *Semiramide,* (which 53 other composers also set to music), Meyerbeer's *L'Africaine,* Delibe's *Lakme,* Verdi's *Aida,* Puccini's *Madama Butterfly* and *Turandot,* to Glass' *Akhnaten* and Adams' *Nixon in China,* the fascination seems to be ever enduring.

The mores and manners of the Ottoman Empire have also been a welcome source for opera plots, especially in the 17th and 18th centuries. In 1683 the Turks laid siege to Vienna. They lost the battle, but the trauma of the event wore off very slowly, changing eventually into a curiosity and even enchantment with that alien culture. Gluck's *Le Cadi Dupé* and *Les Pelerins de la Mecque,* Mozart's *Zaide,* and *L'oca del Cairo,* Rossini's *Il Turco in Italia,* von Weber's *Abbu Hassan,* and of course the subject of this chapter, Mozart's *Die*

Entführung aus dem Serail, all give evidence of the lure of 'Turquoiseries.'

A libretto by Christoph Bretzner, *Belmont und Constanze* set to music by Johann Andre served as basis for Gottlieb Stephanie's book for Mozart's *Entführung.* During the composition of the opera Mozart corresponded as usual at great length with his father. These letters give much insight into his manner of composing, his influence upon the librettist to alter the story for his own purposes, and his eagerness to exploit the vocal prowess of his cast. The latter applied especially to Katharina Cavalieri Constanze (Chapter-opening illustration, 78) and Karl Ludwig Fisher (Osmin). (See 79) His famous statement concerning the poet's role of "obedient servant" to the opera's music, was also made in connection with this composition. The letters in question, dated August 1 and 8, September 26, and October 13, 1781, should be read by anyone involved in a production of this opera. (They appear in an English translation in the third volume of *The Letters of Mozart and his Family* by Emily Anderson.)

Mozart habitually omitted any references to the visual aspects of his (or anyone else's) operas. This was evidently not within the realm of his perception, which is all the more remarkable because his description of Osmin, for one, is so vivid that it is very easy to visualize the character! Luckily, visual records of many 18th-century opera presentations have been preserved for us to investigate and reinterpret. They reveal that mixing Turkish and 18th-century costume elements (80, 81, 82) was 'de rigueur' at that time, a peculiarity which stands today's costumer of the opera in good stead, especially in the case of Constanze, Blonde, and Pedrillo, who by adopting some part of Turkish dress hope to curry favor with their captors.

The music of *Die Entführung* is colorful and its visual production should be no less so. Some designers identify 'Spanish' with 'black,' and consequently costume the Spanish characters Belmonte and Constanze in black. It is true that black was the traditional color for costumes of the Spanish court in the 16th century, but its use remained restricted to that period and those circles. Observing the works of famous Spanish artists like Utrillo, Velasquez, El Greco, Goya, not to mention Dali and Picasso, one finds no preference for the use of black costumes. Neither does the tourist to Spain find such adherence to black clothes among the Spanish people.

Some librettos and programs give the period of the opera as '16th century,' which makes no sense at all. A lithograph has survived of

TOP: Illus. 79; BOTTOM: Illus. 80.

Illus. 81.

Illus. 82.

Mozart conducting a performance of *Die Entführung* in 1782, when the opera had its premiere (83). The two characters visible on the stage, presumably Osmin and Pedrillo, are costumed in Turkish and late 18th-century Spanish attire respectively. For present day productions that is equally valid.

ACT I

From Belmonte's utterances it is apparent that he has already been searching for Constanze a long time. Somehow the music of the overture suggests to this listener that he has been crisscrossing the desert riding on a camel. In reality he has been aboard a ship which is now anchored in the harbor, while the Pasha's summer residence is at the seacoast relatively nearby. Just the same, Belmonte should be in travelling clothes, and one of those 'greatcoats' like the one Mozart is wearing in the aforementioned lithograph, would be just right for him. A bicorn accompanies such a coat, as well as boots. His own black hair is dressed in the queue-back style of the late 18th century. By removing the greatcoat after the opening scene, Belmonte creates the illusion of having a change of costume without returning to the ship, for which there would be no occasion. Underneath the greatcoat Belmonte wears a three-piece suit which has a slightly Spanish flavor (84). It consists of a cutaway coat with a collar, a double-breasted vest with lapels, ankle tights to fit into the boots, lace cuff ruffles and silk stock. This costume has the added advantage of being perfectly acceptable as the attire of the architect he presumes to be.

Our mental concept of a 'Turkish costume,' the actual clothes these people wore, and the 18th-century stage presentations 'a la Turque' rarely coincide. Because an opera production is not a lesson in costume history, a compromise can be reached which will fit the music, the characters, and within reason, the audience's expectations. "Within reason" for it is not absolutely necessary to cater to the audience's lack of knowledge in these matters.

Osmin, the Pasha's overseer, who is referred to by his master as "old man," should wear a substantial pair of Turkish pants, possibly of a patterned fabric, a colored shirt, and an embroidered bolero with some vestiges of hanging sleeves. He wears a prominent waist sash of a contrasting color, usually of a striped fabric (85). The larger his girth

TOP: Illus. 83; BOTTOM: Illus. 84.

the wider the sash. Some years ago a member of the Iranian parliament was seen on television, tearing off his turban in a fit of anger, thereby revealing his bald pate. It seems just the sort of thing Osmin would do, and it must be considered an extreme gesture. Muslims never ever remove their turbans in public. Although Osmin is often portrayed as a man of considerable weight, this does not necessarily have to be so. Portraits of the original Osmin, Karl Fischer, do not give the impression that he was a portly man, nor do some contemporary lithographs. He might even be 'an angry little man.' So long as he is a 'character' the role can have a variety of physical aspects.

Slipper-like footwear is appropriate for Turkish men. To superimpose to these a slightly turned-up toe section in order to achieve that 'turkish' look, should not be too difficult a task. Beards and mustaches were prevalent among Turkish men, and no Osmin should be without them. His are grey, because he is an old man, and straggly to match his character.

Pedrillo, Belmonte's servant, and now the Pasha's gardener, is the next character to appear on the scene. Although there is no mention of his nationality in the libretto, judging from his name he too is Spanish. As such, the Spanish 'majo' costume, so familiar to us from Goya's tapestry designs (and from many Figaro costumes), would be suitable for him, except that he too has borrowed a pair of Turkish pants, and is wearing a fez instead of a snood. A homespun shirt and a gardener's apron complete his outfit (86).

The arrival of Pasha Selim and Constanze from a little ride on the Pasha's pleasure boat, is preceded by another boat carrying the Pasha's Janissaries, his armed guards, who sing a laudatory chorus to their lord. This is a four-part chorus, for sopranos and altos as well as tenors and basses. That leaves one the choice of either costuming the ladies as male Janissaries, or of creating an additional group of female servants, who emerge from the palace to greet the Pasha upon his return, which strikes this writer as the correct solution. Since every Turkish overlord seems to have had his own group of Janissaries (87), their costumes varied from Pasha to Pasha. Above all they must be identical and convey a military feeling. They consist of short Turkish pants with decorated cloth leggings, a colored shirt under an equally decorated bolero. A wide sash holds a curved sabre. Naturally, a turban completes the Janissaries' costume. The physiques of the choristers permitting, the shirts can be omitted. The turban's foundation which is usually red and fez-like, might be of metal in this case,

TOP, LEFT: Illus. 85; TOP, RIGHT: Illus. 86; BOTTOM: Illus. 87.

while some metal trimmings on the bolero might also add to the military look. The serving women who emerge from the palace wear long-sleeved loose-fitting garments over their harem pants, and are heavily veiled (88). Because the veils must cover the mouths, it is essential that its fabric be sheer enough for sound to come through. The servants' garments are not uniforms and can vary in color, so long as the shadings are subtle and they constitute a cohesive group.

'Leisure clothes' as we know them today did not exist in the 18th century. For her pleasure ride aboard the Pasha's yacht Constanze would select from her wardrobe a light-colored bodice and skirt, then called a 'levite,' to which she adds a harem skirt, hoping to appease her captor, and a sheer mantilla-like shawl to protect her black, or possibly auburn tresses, dressed in 18th-century style, from the elements (89).

The Pasha would not undertake such a boat ride dressed in his ceremonial robes. Instead he wears over his Turkish pants a long, light-colored, striped robe, under a patterned short-sleeved long coat (90). A wide sash and a turban are the obligatory accessories. As stands to reason, the size of a turban would vary not merely with the importance of the wearer, but also with the importance of the occasion. An appropriate feather trim might in this case have wafted in the breeze. The Pasha also has a beard and mustache of more imposing dimensions than Osmin's.

ACT II

The much talked about Blonde (91), Constanze's English chambermaid, at last makes her entry in this act. So much emphasis is put on her nationality that an attempt at giving her costume an English flavor is in order. Fortunately the use of plaid fabrics was then in vogue for servant girls in England, and one gladly avails oneself of that fabric for Blonde's bodice and polonaise. Instead of an underskirt she too wears harem pants, of a more modest fabric than Constanze's. Her sheer, short apron will not conceal these. A fichu and mob-cap are of the same fabric. Or might a fez suit her better? That her name was chosen because of the color of her hair is a foregone conclusion.

Constanze's two arias in this act are very different in feeling. The first one is almost a mourning song, while in the second one defiance

TOP, LEFT: Illus. 88; TOP, RIGHT: Illus. 89; BOTTOM, LEFT: Illus. 90; BOTTOM, RIGHT: Illus. 91.

and pleading alternate. A different costume for these different moods seems appropriate. Alas there is no way this can be accomplished. The arias are separated only by dialogue, first between Constanze and Blonde, then between Constanze and the Pasha. She never leaves the stage. One solution to this problem is to cover her now much more formal 'robe à la française,' (92) (though again with harem pants instead of an underskirt), with a large, dark all-enveloping mantilla. She will wear this through the entire 'Traurigkeit' aria only to tear it off in a gesture of defiance at the opening phrase of 'Martern aller Arten.' (93) She might clutch the mantilla to her bosom again in the pleading section of the aria.

Pasha Selim is now also more formally attired in a brocaded robe under a fur-trimmed floor-length coat, with an equally elaborate sash and turban (94).

ACT III

In preparation for the abduction Pedrillo has removed the Turkish elements of his costume as well as his gardener's apron and now wears the complete Spanish Majo costume, snood and all. Klaas, a non-singing character, is the skipper of the escape ship. He is evidently Dutch, Klaas being an abbreviation of the Dutch name Nikolaas. Accordingly he wears navy blue woolen knickers and a waist-length, double-breasted jacket of the same fabric, which reveals at the neck a red-and-white plaid kerchief. He wears a round fur cap, black woolen hose and buckled shoes (95).

Belmonte now returns in his greatcoat, while Constanze wears again her first act costume, but this time with an underskirt instead of the harem pants. A complementary hooded cape is worn over that. Blonde too has relinquished her harem pants for a skirt, while a more modest hooded cape completes her costume. When the four escapees are brought in by the guards, these outer garments will have been removed to indicate that 'they are not going anywhere.'

The mute servant who alerts Osmin, wears a shirt, Turkish pants, a sash and a turban, all rough textured and modest of color (96). The officer sent by Osmin to arouse Pasha Selim, and the four guards who arrest the would-be escapees, wear variations of the Janissaries' costumes. The Pasha repeats his Act II costume, but has added a

TOP, LEFT: Illus. 92; TOP, RIGHT: Illus. 93; BOTTOM, LEFT: Illus. 94;
BOTTOM, RIGHT: Illus. 95.

sword in a 'heads will roll' gesture. If his had been a singing part one wonders how Mozart would have dealt musically with Selim's sudden change of heart.

The Janissaries and serving ladies require no change of costume for their final chorus, although the ladies in particular might benefit from something more festive for the occasion, like short-sleeved bodices of a printed fabric with their harem pants. They must remain veiled, however, in true Moslem tradition! (97)

LEFT: Illus. 96; RIGHT: Illus. 97.

CHAPTER 5

JANACEK'S

Jenufa

Illus. 98

*L*EOS JANACEK, THE COMPOSER of *Jenufa* (or rather: *Her Foster Daughter,* as the play by Gabriela Preissova, on which the opera's libretto is based, was titled) was not merely a Moravian by birth. He was Moravian body and soul. Everything concerning Moravia was intensely important to him. Logically that included its people, their customs, mores, and dress. Since the opera's locale is a village in Moravia, and the cast consists exclusively of inhabitants of that village, the composer imbued every note of the music with a Moravian flavor. Visually the same feeling pervaded the opera's productions. Unfortunately, from a visual point of view, Janacek was not endowed with a sense of theatre. If, for instance two vastly different characters wore identical peasant attire in real life, that is exactly what was duplicated on the stage, in Janacek's productions of *Jenufa.*

It is the function of stage-costumes to underscore its wearer's character and mood, in a manner every listener and spectator can sense. Folk costumes per se will not do that. They are full of significant details which reveal to the insider many aspects of the wearer's status: whether married or single, recently widowed, or how long ago, whether in mourning for a close-, or distant-relative, and so forth. Some costume details will even reveal its wearer's religion. None of these particulars have any theatrical value, yet the composer insisted on absolute authenticity in the productions of *Jenufa*. When, after fourteen years the opera was finally performed in Prague, by the Prague National Theatre the producers decided on a more theatrically valid approach to the opera, especially from the costume point of view. This roused the composer's wrath, which he expressed in angry letters to the opera management.

Oddly enough it is Jenufa herself, who offers the most valid argument concerning the relationship between the look of a costume and the mood of its wearer. For her wedding to Laca she refuses to wear the traditional, strictly prescribed Moravian wedding costume (Chapter-opening illustration, 98) because under the circumstances she does not feel like a bride and hence chooses for the occasion a far simpler dress.

It is equally significant that Janacek, who felt Moravian in every fiber of his body and soul, never wore Moravian dress in civilian life, nor did the members of his family. The explanation for that is a very simple one: People of Janacek's class dressed in fashionable civilian clothes of the period, regardless how Moravian they felt. Such is the power of fashion!

If the composer insisted on absolute authenticity costume-wise, others have gone to the other extreme and dressed the opera in modern clothes, without any reference to its origins. In this chapter the 'Prague' approach has been espoused, which aims at retaining the Moravian milieu, but making it theatrically valid.

ACT I   SCENE 1

In the opening scene of Act I Jenufa is in workday clothes (99), to which she may have added a festive touch in anticipation of Steva's return as a draft rejectee, a circumstance which will permit him to marry her and thus, unbeknownst to him, legitimatize their unborn child.

Illus. 99.

Researchers have established that Moravians' everyday clothes consisted frequently of old, discarded festive ones, which gave their workday appearance a somewhat threadbare festive look. For theatrical purposes it is wise not to emulate this habit, but rather make a clear distinction between work-, and holiday-attire.

One item of dress determined more than anything else the degree of festiveness of a female costume: the number of starched petticoats worn on top of each other, which would ultimately give the skirt an almost barrel-like silhouette (99). It is said that young peasant girls, in the employ of wealthy burghers, were forced to abandon many of those petticoats, because their mistresses objected to the endless hours they would spend, ironing those yards and yards of starched cotton.

Jenufa wears the usual puffed sleeve peasant blouse (100), with its typical split-at-the-elbow bottom flounce, under a laced bodice. These laced bodices (101) play as important a part in Moravians' female costume as they did for two centuries in all European female dress. Their outline and décolletage varied as much as the fabrics of which they were made: from cotton to brocade; or in the ways they were decorated with braid and/or embroideries. They all shared one important characteristic, however: they were always laced middle-front. The quality of the laces and lacing loops matched that of the bodice itself. In Jenufa's case, it may just add that 'festive touch' to her otherwise work-a-day costume. Over a modest number of petticoats Jenufa wears a ballerina-length skirt of a fairly dark, printed fabric, half of which is covered with the equally inevitable apron, of a lighter, but harmonizing printed fabric (102). It is only slightly shorter than the skirt, and may have one or two decorative horizontal stripes near the hem. As a festive touch the apron may be tied to the waist with a fairly wide, embroidered ribbon, with a bow middle-front at the waist, the ends hanging down fairly long.

Peasant headgear (103a,b,c,d) tends to be somewhat more subdued in Moravia than in other parts of Czechoslovakia. Yet here too quite a variety is available for selection: from the simple 'babushka'-like, folded kerchiefs, to much more elaborate concoctions, suitable for grand occasions. Jenufa would be well served here with a pleasingly folded kerchief. It is important that it have hanging ends, for Laca will raise them teasingly with the whip-handle he whittles away at during most of the first scene.

There is also a choice of footwear for Moravian women. Black boots are a favorite and they would also serve Jenufa well. However,

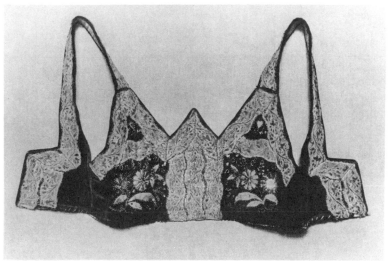

TOP: Illus. 100; BOTTOM: Illus. 101.

Illus. 102.

TOP, LEFT: Illus. 103a; TOP, RIGHT: Illus. 103b; BOTTOM, LEFT: Illus. 103c; BOTTOM, RIGHT: Illus. 103d.

dark hose with 'Mary-Jane' type shoes, pumps, or high-laced shoes (all of them black) have also been observed. A costumer may be hard put to supply a large number of women's black boots. In such cases leatherette boot-tops may be the solution. They are lightweight, can be closed with an (invisible) zipper and must be supplied with two elastics under the shoe, one between heel and sole, and one near the toe region in order to keep the top securely down on the shoe.

It is evident that there are many costume details in Moravian dress which can furnish costumers with the means to express both mood and character through the costumes.

As Kostelnicka's mother-in-law, Jenufa's and Steva's grandmother, and Laca's step-grandmother, Grandmother Burya (104) is the matriarch of the family. It is not clear whether she owns the mill or is its housekeeper, but as the scene opens she is sitting on the porch peeling potatoes. The time is given as 'late September,' so there is not need for winter clothing. Her work clothes consist of a dark, long-sleeved light woolen jacket with a flared peplum. It is modestly decorated with an embroidered band at the outer edges. Underneath it is a high-necked dark blouse. Her ankle-length, ample woolen skirt is of a slightly lighter color, and carries near the hem two bands of decorative braid. The substantial apron might be striped in harmonizing colors. The kerchief of 'married women' pictured here, seems just right for her. Foot- and leg-wear are black.

Laca Klemen (105), grandmother Burya's step-grandson, and Steva's half-brother, feels the 'step-child' in every respect and omits no opportunity to voice these feelings, including his love for Jenufa, who prefers the younger, and handsomer Steva. He is the 'bad guy' who eventually becomes the 'good guy.' Such characteristics are not easily expressed in costume. Naturally his appearance must differ drastically from that of his half-brother. That, during the first act, he is unsuccessfully occupied carving a whip handle, may be considered a subtle psychological touch. He wears dark blue woolen breeches, which are traditionally decorated with a somewhat lighter cord at the thighs, and down the sides. His open-sleeved neck-band shirt has a moderate amount of embroidery at the neck and sleeve bottom. Over it goes an unbuttoned, light brown leather vest. It is moderately decorated with cord at the outer edges and around the buttonholes. The buttons are metal. Like all Moravian men he wears a studded, leather, double belt, which circles the waist once and the second time dips slightly on the right hip. That belt also holds the carving knife, which

TOP: Illus. 104; BOTTOM: Illus. 105.

will be the cause of so much trouble. Black boots, and a moderately brimmed, low-crowned, black-felt hat complete his costume.

Jano, the young shepherd boy (106), next puts in his excited appearance. He seems to be about ten years old, and since the part is written for a soprano voice, it sounds like the ideal role for a boy-soprano. The experts have been unable to explain why that is never done. His breeches of homespun fabric are tucked into short pelt boots. A rough lambskin vest covers his shirt, which is also of homespun fabric, and he wears a small felt hat, with a tapered crown.

SCENES 2 AND 3

The Foreman of the mill, sometimes called 'the Miller,' wears according to the libretto: "a town suit, dusty with flour," a description that seems to have little theatrical validity (107). As the mill's Foreman his costume should have a little more substance than that of the other mill workers, without foresaking a 'Moravian' look. A long coat of lamb's pelt, with the lamb's fur on the inside, would seem just right for him. The front edges are amply decorated with metal studs. The buttons are metal as well, and of substantial size. Over his homespun neck-band shirt, which has its share of embroidery, he wears a tan leather vest, not without a goodly amount of cord decoration, and metal buttons. His boots are of beige pelt, to match his cord-decorated, tight breeches. He would not be without the studded double belt, nor a felt hat with a medium-sized brim. Without going to the trouble of 'dusting his costume with flour,' a somewhat 'floury' look may yet have been achieved in this manner.

At the end of this scene the Kostelnicka appears very briefly. The definite article is purposely added to 'Kostelnicka,' for that is the lady's title, not her name. Her name happens to be Petrona Slamkova, but in the opera she is not once referred to by her name. Her husband Tomas Burya, whose second wife she was, died in an accident after a life of carousing, abuse, and alcohol, leaving her penniless with her young foster daughter Jenufa. The village priest who took pity on her, made her the church's sacristan = Kostelnicka. She is a diligent woman of high moral character, which gives her an aura of severity. She is Jenufa's devoted foster mother. These characteristics set her apart from the other women in the cast, and also influence her

TOP, LEFT: Illus. 106; BOTTOM, RIGHT: Illus. 107.

appearance and hence her costume. Her ankle-length woolen skirt is of the darkest grey, the ample apron of a small cotton print, only a shade lighter. The high-necked blouse is equally somber and closes middle-front with metal buttons (108). In addition she wears a black woolen, peplumed jacket, trimmed at the edges with almost matching braid. The front edges of the jacket, which closes only at the waist, is decorated with silver filigree clasps, which are also placed middle-back, at the waist. Her head covering also differs from that of the other women: over a square, embroidered skull cap, a dark, finely printed kerchief is tied in the back (109). Black boots or high-laced shoes are suggested for Kostelnicka.

SCENES 4, 5, 6, AND 7

In the ensuing scenes the following new characters appear in addition to those who have been described before (except Jano, who will not be seen again until the last act). They are: the Recruits (including Steva; see illustration 110), Musicians, Millworkers (111), and assorted Villagers (112), including some children (113). Among them is Barena, a serving girl at the mill, who has been allotted some solo lines in the last scene.

When they hear the Recruits sing from afar, the above mentioned Millworkers and Villagers hurry on stage, followed by the children. They are all dressed in working clothes. For the men that means: tight-fitting breeches in various shades of light blue, gray, and tan, always with the distinctive studded double belt, and the cord decoration on the thigh. Unbuttoned vests of darker shades are variously decorated. They top the homespun open-sleeved neck-band shirts, with their touches of embroidery. Beige suede boots and the inevitable dark-colored felt hats, with brims of varying widths, and crowns of varying heights, complete their costumes. The women wear light-colored versions of Jenufa's costume, all color-coordinated in order that no one stands out, except Barena, whose apron or kerchief can be more distinctive. The children are dressed in modified miniature versions of their parents' clothes.

The Recruits give the impression of being dressed in uniform, which seems premature for fellows who do not know at the outset of their journey whether or not they will be enlisted. Closer scrutiny

TOP: Illus. 108; BOTTOM: Illus. 109.

TOP: Illus. 110; BOTTOM: Illus. 111.

TOP: Illus. 112; BOTTOM: Illus. 113.

reveals that they are not wearing military uniforms, but civilian festive clothes which are uniform without being 'a uniform' in the military sense. These consist of tight red breeches, all with the peculiar, cord-decorated seam across the buttocks, ending in the familiar thigh decoration. Their black boots frequently carry a decorative tassel hanging from the outside edge. The white shirts have bands of decorations and are topped by an abbreviated, much-decorated vest of green-and-pink brocade. A black felt hat with tapered crown and a tiny rolled brim is profusely decorated with flowered sprigs, topped by some feathers. The traditional studded, double belt is not forgotten either.

The 'musicians' turn out to be 'fiddlers.' (114) Their festive wardrobe, though also uniform in nature, is a much subdued version of the Recruits'. Their breeches are not red, their vests of more normal proportions, and their hats tend to be wide-brimmed, trimmed with one demure flower sprig.

The young women who enter with the Recruits are also in festive attire. Their calf-length pastel-colored skirts are heavily petticoated, and are topped by sheer white, richly embroidered aprons. These are in turn fastened by brocaded ribbons, tied with a bow middle-front, the ends hanging down almost the length of the apron. The laced bodices are lavishly embroidered and decorated in colors that harmonize with the skirts. The puffed sleeves of the blouses have been starched for the occasion, and a deep-pleated ruffle surrounds the throat. Kerchiefs also are more fancy, larger and enriched with fancy embroidery. They are intricately draped over a solid-colored skull cap, with the long end hanging over one shoulder. Hose in complementary colors with black shoes, or black boots, are worn on these occasions.

ACT II

The libretto states that six months have passed since the previous act. In other words, Jenufa was three months pregnant at that time. Yet, no one seems to have noticed her condition, owing perhaps to all those petticoats. Depending on which translation one reads, Jenufa now wears either a 'robe,' (meaning a 'house-robe,' no doubt) or a 'house frock.' The existence of either is highly unlikely in Moravian wardrobes. 'House-robes' were strictly reserved for the upper classes,

Illus. 114.

and bodies and skirts were never of the same fabric, such as constitutes a 'frock.' However, the meaning is clear: a very simple blouse and skirt, of unobtrusive fabric, and but one unstarched petticoat, is what is intended here (115). Her hair may be dressed in a single braid, hanging down the back. When she emerges from her room later in the act, she wears a long, white cotton night gown, with long sleeves and a high neck. Around her shoulders she has a large, knitted, woolen shawl in a light, but not a pastel color.

Kostelnicka may repeat her Act I costume, without the jacket. She, too, has shed several petticoats. Her dark kerchief, without the skull cap underneath, is tied in the simplest manner. When she leaves the house, she wraps herself and the baby in a very large, almost blanket-sized, dark shawl. It is important that at some point during the action the audience may be able to observe the baby's blanket and red cap. It is through these items that Jenufa, in the following act, will identify the dead infant as her child.

During the confrontation with Kostelnicka, Steva (116) is dressed very differently than in Act I. Now it is winter and there is no occasion for festive clothing. With his modestly embroidered neck-band shirt, he wears medium-colored tight breeches with the usual cord decorations, black boots, and the inevitable studded double belt. He also wears a buttoned, tan leather vest with metal ornamentations and tops it all off with a long lambskin coat lined with fur. That coat, too, boasts much metal ornamentation, both front and back. A fur hat completes his costume.

By contrast Laca merely repeats his Act I costume, but adds a heavy dark blue woolen coat lined with lamb's fur.

ACT III

At times, unexpected tragic events can be made to seem doubly disastrous, if they occur unexpectedly at a cheerful and festive occasion. The Wedding Scene in *Lucia di Lammermoor* is a good example of that. In *Jenufa* the situation is quite different. Although its tragic denouement will still come as a shock to all concerned, an atmosphere of gloom pervades this act from the start. Although everyone involved is going through the motions of cheerfulness in one form or another,

TOP: Illus. 115; BOTTOM: Illus. 116.

many reveal their true feelings, if in a roundabout way. Logically, this prevailing mood must also find expression in the costumes.

SCENE 1

The 'Old Shepherdess,' who is arranging Jenufa's hair, has replaced her workday apron and kerchief with some more cheerful ones for this occasion (117, right).

The Mayor's wife remarks that Jenufa's wedding costume (117, left) looks more like that of a widow than that of a bride. Translated into theatrical terms, that might become a combination of light grey and lavender as the basic colors. Accordingly, the skirt is of light grey fabric (possibly a print) with purple-and-lavender horizontal braids near the hem. The apron is of sheer embroidered lavender fabric. Its ties, bow, and hanging ends are of pale green, dull satin ribbon, embroidered in lavender. The white blouse can also have some lavender trim at its sleeve- and throat-ruffles. The laced bodice will consist of lavender brocade trimmed in grey, purple, and silver. It is important that this costume retain an air of simplicity as the libretto indicates. To the horror of the Mayor's wife Jenufa has declined to wear the traditional bridal flower wreath in her hair. A coronet of braided ribbons with a rosette of loops at the nape of the neck, and the ribbon ends hanging down the back, may be a suitable substitute. A moderate number of petticoats and black boots are recommended for this reluctant bride.

Laca too, is a modest bridegroom (118). His long, light grey, cloth coat is trimmed with some grey leather appliques, matching cording and metal buttons. There is some matching grey-braid trimming at the collar and cuff edges. His breeches of grey cloth, a shade lighter than the coat, sport the usual cording and the studded, double belt. The unbuttoned vest is of dark grey leather with metal appliques and buttons, while his boots are black and his small-brimmed black-felt hat has some colored ribbons hanging down the left side and a small flower sprig attached to the crown.

Incidentally, suggestions regarding the sizes of brims and the like are always relative. Opera singers in general, and tenors in particular, are rarely people with small faces. Allowances must always be made

TOP: Illus. 117; BOTTOM: Illus. 118.

for what suits the personality and the figure of a certain performer—
and that applies not merely to hat-brims.

Kostelnicka is wearing again her first act costume, but with a
more festive apron and kerchief (119). In her condition, that is all the
effort she can muster.

Grandmother Burya also has replaced her first act apron and
kerchief for more festive ones. She is simply too old to bother with
any further changes. (The costume budget may be too tight as well.)

SCENE 2

The Mayor and his wife attend the weddings that take place in
their village. It is a routine affair for them and no great shakes. The
Mayor has donned his official 'uniform' for such occasions (120, 121).
It consists of a long coat of dark blue cloth, with a shoulder-cape. He
wears this as a 'cape-coat' draped over his shoulders. The coat is
lavishly embroidered at the stand-up collar, the cuffs, the pockets and
around the buttonholes. The buttons are also of various colors to
match the embroidery. The coat's ample shoulder cape, which has fine
pipe-pleating in the back, from shoulder to shoulder, is also trimmed
with light blue embroidery. The brim of his matching, dark-blue felt,
bicorn hat, is rolled up on either side. The edge is bound by a colored
braid, which also circles the pushed-in crown, the ends hanging down
the middle-back, and from the right side of the crown. His dark blue,
unbuttoned vest is embroidered all over in colors that match those on
the coat. The breeches are bright red, with a lavishly embroidered front
flap and single belt. The white neckband shirt has plenty of light-blue
embroidery as well. The edges of his black boots dip to a corner in
front, and are piped in red, with red decorative tabs hanging down the
sides. An umbrella of a patterned red fabric plus a matching handkerchief complete his costume.

The Mayor's wife (122) knows what is the proper attire for a
woman of her position, as well as what is proper for anyone else in
that respect, as her disapproving remarks about Jenufa's wedding dress
indicate. Although she does not mean to be outdone by her husband's
sartorial splendor, she also knows that it is her place to play second
fiddle. Therefore, she wears a tailored light-blue cloth coat trimmed
from top to bottom with black fur banding, including the pockets and

TOP: Illus. 119; BOTTOM, LEFT: Illus. 120; BOTTOM, RIGHT: Illus. 121.

the cuffs. From the waist down the coat splits open revealing the embroidered apron over a maroon skirt. A wide lace ruffle protrudes from the fur collar to frame her face. It barely reveals the simply draped kerchief over an embroidered skull cap. Her other accessories are black boots and a printed handkerchief. She does not skimp on petticoats.

SCENE 3

Laca pins a small bouquet of flowers to Jenufa's bodice. Otherwise both repeat their previous costumes in this scene.

SCENE 4

Karolka, the Mayor's daughter and Steva's fiancee, expresses the mixed emotions of both in her opening phrases. It seems that Steva displayed his misgivings by delaying their arrival through undue tardiness, while she feels inexplicably sad and is depressed by the lack of music at the wedding. Nevertheless, both are dressed for the occasion. Under a medium green, long cloth coat, trimmed with cording and metal buttons, worn like a cape-coat, Steva wears dark blue breeches, with their usual trim and belts. Over the open-sleeved, embroidered neckband shirt he wears a loose, unbuttoned red vest, trimmed with cording around the edges, buttonholes, and pocket flaps, and the buttons are made of metal as usual. His boots and stiff-brimmed hat are black. The latter has a tapered crown, circled by a brocaded ribbon, the ends of which hang down over the edge in the back.

Karolka (123) follows her mother's example in wearing a tailored, beige cloth coat, trimmed with bandings of light brown fur. The jacket is shorter than Mama's and hence reveals more of the embroidered apron and the peach-colored skirt under it. The number of her petticoats are respectable, but not extreme. She too wears a neck ruffle, a kerchief draped over a skull cap, and black boots.

SCENE 5

There are no costume changes in this scene.

Illus. 122.

SCENE 6

Barena and the Village girls have come to flower bouquets to Jenufa and to sing to her. They point out that they were not invited. Hence, they are not in festive dress. They merely exchanged their workday aprons and kerchiefs for their Sunday-best ones and pinned a rosette with flowing ribbons to their shoulders as a festive touch.

SCENES 7 TO 12

The cast all repeat their previous costumes. In the final scene Jenufa and Laca bring this woeful story yet to a happy end.

Illus. 123.

CHAPTER 6

Illus. 124

WAGNER'S

Lohengrin

WAGNER DREW UPON MANY sources for his libretto of *Lohengrin*. The poet Wolfram von Eschenbach (the author of *Parzival*) and several other medieval sources are cited, some German, some French. The only character in the opera who can be traced historically is King Heinrich (The Fowler) of Germany, who died in 936 A.D. This date establishes the era of the opera's action. King Heinrich's problems with the invading Hungarians, the support he received from the Saxonians, as well as the defeat of the Danes by the Brabantians have been historically substantiated. Everything else in the libretto is poetic invention.

The costumes of the 10th century are of a simplicity which does not harmonize with Wagner's ornate orchestration. Furthermore there are in the opera's text several references to 'sumptuous garments,' which one is hard put to discover among 10th-century clothes. Reaching back to some elements of the richly ornamented late-

Byzantine styles—and forward as far as the 13th century—will enable a producer to conceive a harmonious early-medieval look which suits the story as well as the music without going to the extreme of supplying Elsa and Ortrud with hoop skirts (125), as was done in Wagner's own time.

How knowledgeable Wagner himself was in matters of costume is a moot question. In the text he describes Lohengrin upon his first appearance as 'a Knight in shining Armor,' (Chapter-opening illustration, 124) a look one usually associates with tournament participants of a much later date. Matters of this kind have to be carefully weighed and balanced in order to achieve a production that does visual justice to the music and the story.

In the opening scene of the opera the libretto indicates that King Heinrich is surrounded by Counts and Nobles of the Saxonian militia (126). (The index also lists Thuringian Nobles, but they are never mentioned again.) The King and his retinue have come to Antwerp, in Brabant, for various reasons. It must be evident from their appearance that they have been travelling, and although they carry swords, shields, and spears they are not in armor. Complete armor was only worn in battle and the only ones so attired are Lohengrin upon his first and final appearances and Count Friedrich von Telramund on the occasion of his duel with Lohengrin. In this respect it is curious to observe the score's stage direction, just before that duel takes place, which reads: "Lohengrin and Friedrich complete putting on their armor." It is an odd remark because neither had the opportunity to don or doff anything since their first entrance.

ELSA

Elsa von Brabant is a symbol of purity and innocence, characteristics which in dress are represented by the color 'white.' It is logical, therefore, that Elsa is clad in white, although the stage directions do not mention her being so attired until Act II, Scene 2. which might indicate that she is not necessarily always dressed in white. If not white then it must be another very light shade, like pale blue, a color which is usually associated with the Madonna for that very reason. None of these colors have the reputation of being slenderizing to the figure of the average soprano who can cope successfully with the vocal demands of Elsa's music. Yet white or pale blue it must be and it is, therefore, up to the costumer's ingenuity to devise a set of flattering garments for our heroine in these shades. Luckily medieval gowns are usually cut in the 'princess style,' without a seam at the waist which is helpful in this respect. Decorative bands (127) may be applied vertically thereby producing a slenderizing effect. It is logical also that for this outdoors scene Elsa wears a floor-length cape with a slight train. The cape opens middle-front, falls straight down from each side of the neck and is bordered by a decorative band. It is held in place by an invisible strap which is attached on the inside at the shoulder and continues under the armpit to close in the middle back. In the region of the arm the cape can either be shortened to uncover the hands or it can be draped in folds at the elbow region for that purpose. Lining the cape in a very light, but contrasting color will also produce a slenderizing effect. A contrast in fabric-texture between gown and cape is also helpful in that respect, as well as a hairdo with long braids or ribbon-bound hair on either side of the face. The hair is partly covered by a sheer wimple, under a jewelled coronet.

Footwear was strictly of the slipper-type, but invisible platforms can be used for the purpose of giving height, or to comfort those who feel ill at ease in heel-less shoes.

Elsa's wedding gown (128) must be a two-part invention. Before the wedding ceremony she appears on the balcony in what might be a glorified version of her first act dress, now definitely in white. A white-on-white brocade is suggested. If the brocade happens to have a bit of silver in it, so much the better. The vertical ornamental bands are now far more elaborately adorned with jewelled stones and pearls. These bands have a loose outer edge, thereby creating the illusion of a tabard. The overgarment is actually a long bridal train, whose ornamental border matches that of the gown. It will be attached to the gown at the shoulder by jewelled ornaments and thus create the illusion that the ornamental band on the gown continues into the train. Elsa's sheer and substantial bridal veil may also have some silver woven into it, while the coronet consists of white-jewelled flowers. The train as well as the wedding veil will be removed by some pages after the ceremony in the bridal chamber. It is important, therefore, that her hairdo will still pass muster after the veil is removed, in order to function in the following important scene. A simple silver head band underneath the coronet may accomplish that.

Illus. 125.

Illus. 126.

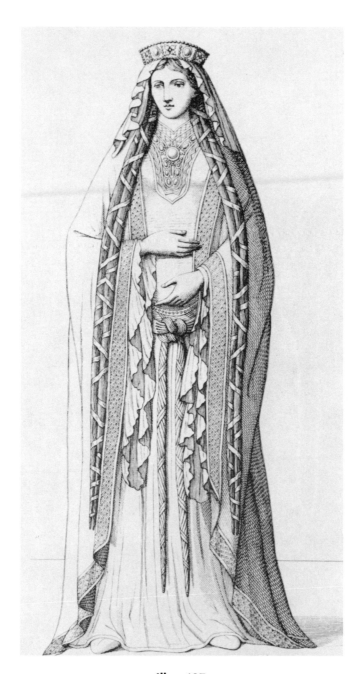

Illus. 127.

Illus. 128.

After the fatal encounter with Telramund, Lohengrin directs two of Elsa's ladies to get her suitably attired for the ensuing meeting with King Heinrich. It must become evident in her costume that as a result of Ortrud's evil manipulations Elsa's innocence has been tainted. Over her first act white gown she now wears a mantle with three-quarter length wide sleeves of a sheer, greyish-gold fabric, again decorated with richly ornamented bands. There is a matching sheer wimple and coronet.

Because Elsa is constantly sinking to her knees, unto Lohengrin's bosom, or fainting, it is important that the fabrics of all her garments are of a limp texture. One does not faint very gracefully in stiff fabrics.

ORTRUD

Ortrud is evil personified. There are no redeeming features to her character and in this opera Lohengrin, Elsa, Gottfried and Telramund all are her victims. The kind of revenge she will wreak upon poor little Gottfried in retaliation for the events that took place in this opera, would provide suitable material for another libretto.

Ortrud's evil character is best expressed costume-wise through a severe gown of steel grey lame, over which various sheer garments are worn to suit different occasions, as well as to express her varying aims and moods. Furthermore, while all other garments of this large cast are strictly symmetrical in design, hers—and to a lesser extent Telramund's—are asymmetrical (129), which symbolizes that character-wise there is something awry. In her first appearance Telramund introduces his wife to King Heinrich. Naturally she wants to impress the King favorably and is accordingly all done up for the occasion. Since Telramund makes much of her noble Frisian ancestry, it is suggested that her cape of dark brocade, which closes asymmetrically on one shoulder with a jewelled clasp, is richly decorated with heraldic devices representing her noble house. Her jewelled tiara and wimple are also dark hued.

After Telramund's initial defeat Ortrud pulls her 'sackcloth and ashes' stunt in her appearance before Elsa. The stage directions describe her and Telramund's looks on this occasion as "knechtisch," which is best translated as 'servile.' A tattered, sheer, asymmetrically-draped overgarment in various shades of dark brown and dark grey,

Illus. 129.

with a complementary headband and wimple will accomplish that. At the same time, however, there must be something slyly seductive about her looks which may be produced through the application of some veiled glitter. After all, Elsa falls for the act and promises Ortrud that the latter will attend her wedding clad in "splendid robes." (130) In these robes Ortrud plays her great defiance scene, and her costume must reflect that attitude as well. A sheer, orangey-red garment over the steel grey lame, topped by an asymmetrical cape resembling a multicolored stained-glass window, with complementary tiara and wimple, might just accomplish that. In the opera's final scene Ortrud can repeat the previous costume, but without the cape, or she might tear off the cape in a gesture of despair upon Gottfried's emergence.

FEMALE CHORUS

All the female chorus members are Brabantians. The score defines their status as: Elsa's Women and as Inhabitants of the Castle, later on referred to as The People. Furthermore there are two non-singing 'Maids' who precede Elsa with 'lights' (one assumes, 'candles') in Act II, Scene 2. The size of the production and the size of the budget will determine which is the best way to costume these ladies. It would be nice to give Elsa's 'Women' (131, 132) (evidently her 'retinue,' some kind of 'ladies in waiting') a complete change of costume when, after their initial appearance, they accompany Elsa as a bride, and are according to the stage directions "magnificently attired." On the other hand it is possible to add to their initial gowns certain elements which will give the impression of a total transformation while not totally depleting the budget. When they enter with Elsa for the first time, an assortment of simple medieval cloth gowns in various subdued related colors is in order. A variety of short wimples with circlets, coifs with chinstraps (the latter cut on the bias in order not to impede vocalism) or gorgets, are suitable headdresses to go with such gowns. An occasional supplementary cape is not out of order either. These ladies must not look like a chorus line, but rather like individuals who (for theatrical purposes) interrelate. Their transformation into bridal magnificence can be accomplished through the use of brocaded surcoats. 'Mi-parti' treatment, the application of heraldic devices as well as ornamental bands, all will serve to

TOP: Illus. 130; BOTTOM, LEFT: Illus. 131; BOTTOM, RIGHT: Illus.
132.

reinforce a rich and festive look. For this event their headgear has also blossomed forth into far more substantial wimples, chinbands, coifs, and coronets (133). Ortrud who on this occasion pretends to be one of them should yet stand out, but not as the proverbial 'sore thumb.' The asymmetrical cape may achieve that.

Eight ladies from this group are singled out as 'brides maids.' Their surcoats, identical in cut, are made of assorted pastel brocades, while their wimples and floral coronets must be identical. The female members of 'the people' are naturally of many different ages, which their clothes should emphasize. Their dresses are ankle length, of homespun fabrics, in assorted subdued colors—darker for the old folks and lighter for the young ones. Their headdresses also vary with age. Young girls can wear their hair in braids with a simple chin- and/or headband, while short wimples, gorges, cauls, and so forth, are suitable for older women. A differentiation in social status can also be accomplished through the choice of distinguishing fabrics and the modest application of ornamentation. The costumes of the candles-carrying maids are like those of the middle-class people, but theirs should be identical.

KING HEINRICH

A cue to King Heinrich's attire is the frequent mention of his 'shield.' (134) The only civilian in the cast who carries a shield is the Herald in his capacity as the King's voice. For all others the bearing of a shield is an indication of military dress, unlike swords, which were carried by many civilians and all military. The basic element of military dress was 'chainmail,' which was initially metal rings sewn unto leather or heavy linen (135). Eventually these rings would be interlinked. Leggings, sleeves, tunics, hoods, and gauntlets were all fashioned from chainmail. Other parts of the costume were superimposed on it, like helmets, cloth tunics, metal breastplates, and parts of leg- and sleeve-armor. The metal used for chainmail also varied, from iron to silver and even gold, depending on the social position of the wearer as well as the importance of the occasion. A King would not wear gold chainmail into battle, but he might wear it for a ceremonial event. King Heinrich came to Antwerp on a diplomatic mission and became only incidentally involved in the judgment of Elsa. It is,

TOP: Illus. 133; BOTTOM: Illus. 134.

therefore, reasonable to assume that he wore dark silver chainmail leggings and sleeves, a three-quarter length woolen, or velvet tunic, decorated with ornamental bands and metal studs. The chainmail hood is topped by a jewelled crown. A jewelled belt carries an equally jewelled sheath containing a sword with a jewelled sword handle. Over it all goes a heavy floor-length cape, edged in fur and with an ornamental jewelled band going along the front edge and bottom hem. High across the chest it is held together by a horizontal jewelled band. Like Elsa's cape it has to be shaped so as not to impair his arm movements, since he must be able to hang his shield on the judgment tree, as the stage directions indicate. That shield bears the escutcheons of Saxony and the King's own lineage, elaborately executed. To attend the ensuing wedding ceremony, all chainmail is removed from the King's attire. Underneath the same cape he now wears a splendidly decorated full length, long-sleeved brocaded robe. With this he wears the crown directly on his head.

LOHENGRIN

In the score's text the costume Lohengrin wears upon his arrival is precisely described (136). It states that "the eye is blinded by the sheen of his armor," while further on it enumerates his: "shining silver armor, a helmet on his head, a shield on his back, a small golden horn at his side, while he leans on his sword." Most tenors capable of dealing with the role's vocal demands are physically no shrinking violets and might look twice their size decked out in this fashion. However, tricks of the costumer's trade when deftly applied will make it possible to costume him as described and yet make him look attractively presentable. In the development toward full-fledged metal armor, it became the habit to put pieces of metal on top of chainmail in strategic places. Exactly this method should be pursued in devising Lohengrin's costume, which basically consists of a tunic, sleeves, and leggings of shiny silver chainmail. The aforementioned metal plates can then be placed on all these items in a fashion to create a slenderizing effect. A draped silver cloth-armhole cloak will also create a slenderizing impression, while at the same time disguising the full extent of the swordbelt around his waist. The traditional swan's wings on his helmet can be dispensed with.

TOP: Illus. 135; BOTTOM: Illus. 136.

As regards Lohengrin's wedding costume (which he evidently brought along 'just in case'), over white tights he wears a pair of white leather 'chausses.' (137) Chausses were medieval forerunners of boots. Occasionally they were richly decorated, but Lohengrin preferred his to be nice and simple. A white brocade calf-length tunic may be topped by a silver brocade tabard—which is entirely open at the sides—thus revealing part of the silver sword belt underneath. The tabard may carry a swan emblem on the chest. On top of all this goes a floor-length white velvet cape, open in the middle-front, trimmed with jewelled bands and closed on the chest with a jewelled clasp. After the ceremonies in the bridal chamber, pages will relieve him of this cape. Upon his departure from the shores of the river Scheldt, he wears again the costume of his initial appearance.

TELRAMUND

As the Count of Brabant, Telramund's costume (138) may stand out somewhat from that of the other Nobles of Brabant. He is entirely under Ortrud's evil spell which has also influenced his appearance. He wears chainmail sleeves and leggings of the darkest shade of steel, with a knee-length tunic composed of leather strips of the same color. His swordbelt, sword, and sheath are of the same hue, as are his helmet and metal gorget. His asymmetrically-closed cape, slightly lighter in color has decorated borders (139). His 'servile' look is achieved by replacing his grey cape with a solid black one, which is asymmetrically draped to cover him entirely. He should also remove his helmet for the occasion. For his duel with Lohengrin and the final attack, he wears a dark metal harness plate.

THE HERALD

Heralds are usually young men of no great dramatic impact who are visually mostly ornamental (140). In this opera the Herald is part of King Heinrich's retinue. He is an adult, and as the King's representative and in a way, his voice, his is a role of considerable substance, which deserves to be costumed accordingly. With a chainmail tunic, sleeves, and leggings, a calf-length, short-sleeved mi-parti tabard is

TOP: Illus. 137; BOTTOM, LEFT: Illus. 138; BOTTOM, RIGHT: Illus. 139.

suggested, which is open at the sides and bears the Saxonian coat of arms both front and back. Under a brimmed helmet he wears a chainmail hood, and he carries a shield which also displays the Saxonian coat of arms.

GOTTFRIED

The stage directions indicate that Gottfried appears in shining silver attire, and so it shall be (141). Since he does not sing care must be taken to cast a likely looking lad in the part with a good figure. Over a silver leotard he wears a silver brocade tabard, which is belted only in front but forms a cape-like loose hanging panel in the back. His silver shoes have silver straps crossing up his legs. He wears a silver crown on his blond curls.

THE MALE CHORUS

What was said regarding the size of the production and the size of the budget relative to the Female Chorus is even more valid in the case of the Male Chorus, which plays such a prominent part in this opera. Careful scrutiny of the score reveals that its participants fill a number of roles, to wit: Saxonian Counts and Nobles of the Saxonian militia. Brabantians of their kind are also present in abundance. The male equivalent of 'inhabitants of the castle' or 'The People' (142) are on the scene as well. Some subtle subdivisions are mentioned, especially among the Saxonians, such as the spear carriers, who function as seconds during the Lohengrin-Telramund duel, but there are no indications that this constitutes a difference in costume.

It is important to give the Saxonians and the Brabantians each their own costume flavor. The Saxonians, because they are travelling should have a more armorial look about them (143). To their steel-grey chainmail leggings and sleeves they add grey leather tunics, decorated with studded metal ornaments. Conical metal helmets cover chainmail hoods, and chainmail gauntlets have metal cuffs. Sheathed swords are attached to leather belts. Each man carries an elbow-high shield. Shields formed an important part of medieval noblemen's attire. They were made in various shapes: round, oval, and kite-

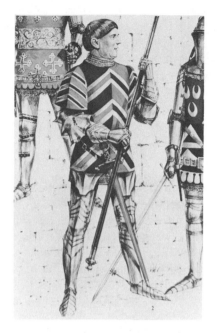

TOP: Illus. 140; BOTTOM: Illus. 141.

shaped. The latter form is now generally identified with the shape of a shield. Shields were frequently decorated with the bearer's coat of arms. Round shields seem appropriate for the Saxonians, while kite-shaped ones will suit the Brabantians. Lohengrin's shield could be oval for the sake of variety and because he carries it on his back. To set apart the Saxonian Counts from the mere Nobles, the former wear draped woolen capes of matching colors, which are attached at the shoulder underneath the gorgets of their chainmail hoods. The Brabantians also wear chainmail leggings and sleeves of a somewhat lighter steel grey than the Saxonians. Their thigh-long hauberks are of wool and can be of various related colors. The Brabantian Counts wear matching woolen capes as well. On top of their chainmail hoods they wear round-top helmets. Their gauntlets have no metal cuffs, while leather belts support their sheathed swords. The four Nobles who abet Telramund in his sneak attack on Lohengrin may have donned breastplates for the occasion.

The Brabantian male populace (144a,b,c) wear rough homespun tunics in earthy tones, varying in length, color, and quality according to their age and standing in society. Some wear hooded cowls, others skull caps, coifs, or are bare-headed. Their woolen tights, or leggings are cross-strapped with leather straps, which attach to their slipper-like leather shoes.

TRUMPETERS

Aside from Gottfried, the four Trumpeters are the most important non-singing characters in this opera. With their chainmail leggings and sleeves they wear short-sleeved mi-parti tabards revealing the Saxonian coat of arms. Their heads are covered with brimmed felt hats with spiked crowns, on top of woolen chaperons.

PAGES

One assumes that the Page boys are part of the Brabantian realm. Because the four among them who sing are identified as sopranos and altos they must be of the female gender, unless boy-sopranos and boy-altos can musically fill the bill. All the others can be young

TOP: Illus. 142; BOTTOM: Illus. 143.

TOP, LEFT: Illus. 144a; TOP, RIGHT: Illus. 144b; BOTTOM: 144c.

fellows. In true mi-parti fashion each leg of their tights is of a different color, as are each of their sleeves. Their thigh-length, sleeveless tunics are quartered in similar fashion and bear the Brabantian coat of arms (145). Their page boy coiffures require no headgear.

SERVANTS

The male servants who appear at the opening of Act II, Scene 3 in order to perform various tasks, do not seem to be in livery or uniform. Accordingly they are dressed like the simpler members of the male populace (146, 147).

Illus. 145.

TOP: Illus. 146; BOTTOM: Illus. 147.

CHAPTER 7

DONIZETTI'S

Lucia di Lammermoor

Illus. 148

*I*N ACT II–SCENE ONE of the opera, Enrico Ashton says to his sister Lucia: "William is dead–We shall see Mary take the throne. . . ." The 'William and Mary' he is talking about are William III of Orange and his wife Mary II Stuart, who were crowned King and Queen of England in 1689. Cammarano, Donizetti's librettist for this opera, is mistaken in this. Mary could not become William's successor for two reasons: William and Mary were crowned joint sovereigns, in other words, she was already on the throne. The second reason is even more compelling: William died in 1702 in the arms of his lover Hans Willem Bentinck, Earl of Portland. Mary had died eight years previously in 1694. William was succeeded by Mary's half-sister Anne, a lady immortalized by a style of 18th-century English furniture, named after her. Despite these slips of the mind it is clear that the librettist intended the opera to take place during the reign of William and Mary, and accordingly it should be costumed in the fashions of those days.

With those fashions we are familiar. They were in the style mainly identified with King Louis XIV of France. Although William was Louis' most powerful adversary, he wore a 'Justaucorps' (149) just as Louis did, while Mary sported a 'Fontange' (150) like Mme. de Maintenon, Louis' mistress (to mention but two outstanding costume features of that time). It tells us a great deal about the power of 'fashion.' Personal animosity has never resulted in a rejection of the fashionable attire by one of the parties involved. Peoples have waged the most devastating wars against each other, yet have continued to adhere to wearing the same clothes fashionable at that time. 'Sumptuary Laws' whose purpose it was to regulate 'who was allowed to wear what,' or rather, 'who was NOT allowed to wear what,' have been notoriously unsuccessful throughout history.

Possibly because the fashions of William and Mary's time are so closely identified with Louis XIV, *Lucia* is never costumed in that period. The time usually chosen instead is the third quarter of the 17th century. The events on which Sir Walter Scott based his novel *The Bride of Lammermoor* took place in 1668, which evidently motivated this choice of time for the opera's setting. Yet even that period has not been universally adopted. Many productions choose the 16th century for the opera's era. Furthermore, Cammaratno's libretto so transforms Sir Walter's novel, that the validity of adopting either period becomes questionable.

As a way out of the confusion this writer once chose 1835, the year of the opera's first performance for its setting and hence for its costumes. With a few changes in the text, it worked like a charm and is therefore advocated here.

One element frequently overlooked in the costuming of *Lucia* is the circumstance that the opera takes place in Scotland, where especially among people of the upper classes 'Highland Dress' (151) was generally adopted (except between 1746 and 1782, when, with little success, an Act of Parliament forbade its wear in Scotland). Sir Walter was a strong advocate of the use of Highland Dress in the dramatizations of his novels which had Scotland as its locale. This implies, of course, the wearing of 'kilts' (152) for the gentlemen, something opera singers do not unanimously subscribe to (although the celebrated Caruso (153) did not object to baring his knees on that occasion). Luckily there is an alternative to 'kilts,' to wit, 'trews.' (154) Originally they were an almost 'tights'-like leg covering made of tartan cloth, cut on the bias, which eventually developed into 'tartan pants'

TOP, LEFT: Illus. 149; TOP, RIGHT: Illus. 150; BOTTOM, LEFT: Illus. 151; BOTTOM, RIGHT: Illus. 152.

Illus. 153.

cut on the straight (155). They are part of the uniform of many Scottish regiments in the British army, and can for costuming purposes be used for civilian wear as an alternative to kilts. Tartan cloth is an important part of Highland Dress and specific patterns and colors are identified with individual clans. Since 'Ravenswood' and 'Ashton' are not among the clans thus identified, it is suggested that these colors and patterns be used in the opera's costumes rather for the purpose of characterization and to underline a mood. Thus one can use a 'happy' tartan or a 'sad' tartan wherever such is suitable.

The male Highland costume (156) changed very little through the ages. On pictures of days gone by, the man's fashionable hairdo is often the only identification to the time of its origin. The costume consisted of kilts or trews of tartan cloth, a single-breasted jacket, some times a single-breasted vest, a shirt with fashionable neckwear, sporrans, a belt and sword, and a Scottish tam.

Initially the left-over length of cloth used to pleat the kilt, was thrown as a plaid (157) over the left shoulder, sometimes held there by a silver clasp. Later on, the kilt and plaid were separated, but it remained an important part of the costume, even when trews replaced the kilt. Plaids were ever present for outdoor wear. Men would wrap themselves in them in various ways, depending on mood, circumstances, and weather conditions. The jacket (158) was always single-breasted and conformed to the prevailing fashions, although its 18th-century form predominates to this day: cuffed, short-skirted, with side-flaps surmounted by pocket-flaps, and with metal buttons. At times the jackets are belted with the so-called 'Dirk Belt,' closed with an ornamented silver buckle. The 'Dirk' is an ornamented dagger suspended from this belt. Vests, worn with unbelted styles only, varied with the fashions, but were always single-breasted. Shirts and neckwear also conformed to fashion, but for evening wear lace jabots and modest cuff ruffles persisted.

Because neither kilts nor the original trews could accommodate pockets, a 'sporran,' (159) initially a leather bag, was suspended from the waist. When the trews developed into narrow pants, there was room for pockets and hence no further need for sporrans.

The 'Balmoral Bonnet' (160-2) a solid-colored tam, is the most common outdoor head covering, although the kepi-like 'Glengarry Bonnet' (160-1) is also popular, especially for military purposes. Both

TOP: Illus. 154; BOTTOM: Illus. 155.

TOP, LEFT: Illus. 156; BOTTOM, RIGHT: Illus. 157.

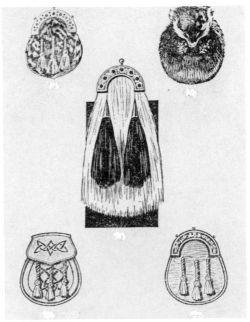

TOP, LEFT: Illus. 158; BOTTOM, RIGHT: Illus. 159.

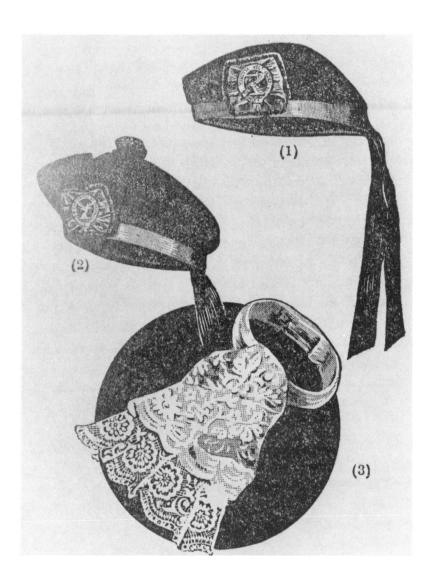

Illus. 160 (1,2,3).

Illus. 161.

have ribbon streamers (160-3) down the middle-back, while a 'cap-badge' (161) is attached to the left side of the bonnet.

'Highland' ladies' dress was much less complicated. It consisted of a fashionable dress over which for outdoor purposes a very large plaid could be worn. For indoor wear the plaid was reduced to shawl-like proportions, while for evening fashions it shrank to a narrow tartan band, as will be described in more detail later.

ACT I SCENE 1

Normanno is the captain of Enrico Ashton's guards. As such a uniform-type Highland Dress is in order for him. He is a sinister character, which should be reflected in his costume. It consists of a black woolen military jacket of the period with metal buttons, epaulettes, a Dirk-Belt and sword, plus a matching Balmoral Bonnet. His trews and plaid are in the dark green, purple, and yellow Tartan of the Farquarson Clan.

The chorus of 'Huntsmen,' (162) who sing such a jolly tune to a rather somber text, can wear identical dark brown tweed jackets to the dark brown and beige Tartan of the Scott Clan for their trews and plaid. Matching Glengarry Bonnets and rifles will complete their costumes.

Enrico Ashton is the opera's 'wicked man' as Raimondo calls him, although he does express remorse after it is too late. His jacket and Balmoral Bonnet are of dark green wool, to go with his trews and plaid in the Tartan of the Keith Clan. He also wears a Dirk-Belt and a Dirk.

It is not easy to ascertain what was worn by Presbyterian Ministers like Raimondo (163) when they were not officiating. The annals of ecclesiastical vestments do not deem their simple attire worthy of description and no snapshots of that period have survived. Luckily some cartoonists have made Ministers the butt of their satire and especially Charles Williams portrayed one in 1824 as wearing a fashionable black woolen coat over a matching high-buttoned vest, black woolen knee breeches, and white clerical tabs. For outdoor purposes a stiff black beret, worn absolutely straight, and black cloth leggings were added to his black buckled shoes, as well as a black cape. All the buttons of this outfit were made of self-fabric.

TOP, LEFT: Illus. 162; BOTTOM, RIGHT: Illus. 163.

ACT I   SCENE 2

Lucia wears a fashionable but simple daytime dress (See chapter-opening illustration, 148). So much mention is made of her mother's recent death, that a degree of mourning is essential in her appearance, wherefore a very dark purple fabric is suggested. With that she wears an ample plaid, which can be of a somewhat more vivid color. She is after all a girl in love. The purple, grey, and red Tartan of the Murray of Atholl Clan seems appropriate for that.

Alisa, Lucia's servant and companion, wears a dark grey, Puritan-type dress (164) with a large, very dark-beige apron. A white collar and servant's cap complete her outfit. For this outdoor occasion she also wears a plaid. The subdued Tartan of the Mackay Clan seems proper for her.

Edgardo's jacket and Balmoral Bonnet (165) are of dark blue wool to harmonize with the lighter blue background of the Tartan of the Elliot Clan which will serve for his trews and plaid. He too wears a Dirk-Belt and a Dirk.

The choice of tartans named here is of necessity an arbitrary one and is to be interpreted merely as a guideline. The overall color scheme of the scene, performers' characteristics, and the availability of fabrics all influence such decisions. The tartans, described by their Clans' names, are depicted in many books. In this instance Lorna Black's *Clans and Tartans, the Fabric of Scotland* (New York: Gallery Books, W. H. Smith Inc., Publishers) was used. The colors are mentioned in addition to the Clans' names, because many Clans availed themselves of various tartans.

ACT II   SCENE 1

Normanno repeats his Act I costume, but does not wear the plaid indoors.

Enrico, too, could repeat his first act costume, or he might change his trews to the Tartan of somewhat more vivid colors of the Macalpine Clan, so that by comparison Lucia may seem even paler. It will furthermore support his angry mood.

A point is made of Lucia's listlessness and pallor (166). A dress of a very faint tartan fabric, the background of which almost matches

TOP, LEFT: Illus. 164; BOTTOM, RIGHT: Illus. 165.

her skin-tone, can accomplish that. A shoulder shawl of the Westpoint Tartan will complete her costume.

Raimondo has shed his outdoors cape, beret, and leggings, but otherwise repeats his Act I costume.

ACT II   SCENE 2

Enrico intends Lucia's wedding to be a festive occasion. All the attendants, guards, retainers, servants, lackeys, etc., are in gala attire. The guests too are in their gayest and most elegant party clothes. There must be no visual anticipation of the dire events that will ensue. On the contrary, in such happy and festive surroundings these events will seem doubly calamitous.

The libretto makes no mention of Normanno's presence in this scene, but it is unthinkable that he would be absent especially since the Guards, whose Captain he is, are on the scene. He repeats his Act I costume, sans plaid, while his underlings wear uniforms identical to his, except for shoulderstraps instead of epaulettes and Glengarry Bonnets instead of his Balmoral one. Dirk-Belts and Dirks are worn by all Guards.

How many supers like the aforementioned lackeys etc., will be used in this scene depends to a large extent on the size of the production, the stage, and the budget. Some stage-directors seek safety in numbers. The more people there are on the stage, the better they like it. It is a misconception costumers must learn to reckon with.

Lackey uniforms consist of lightly-brocaded cutaway coats, solid-colored harmonizing breeches, and vests (167). Coats and vests can be moderately trimmed with braid. White hose, buckled shoes, jabots, and cuff ruffles are necessary additions, as well as white queue wigs and white gloves.

'Retainers' may be all sorts of things. For this occasion one may opt for 'Major Domos,' who are one grade above lackeys, as are their costumes in fabric and trim. They can have an 'aiguillette' on the right shoulder, which in this case may be two narrow loops of tartan cloth (168).

There is no mention in the libretto at what time of day the wedding ceremony takes place. From the fact that directly thereafter the newlyweds retire to their sleeping quarters, one may assume that

TOP, LEFT: Illus. 166; BOTTOM, RIGHT: Illus. 167.

this is an evening affair, where the guests expect to feast till the wee hours. The advantage of this timing is that it is much easier, especially for the lady guests, to produce a gala look in evening clothes (169, left) than in daytime attire. Now they will be dressed in an array of gay and fashionable evening gowns, with flattering décolletages, a display of jewelry, flowered hair-arrangements, and since this is after all Scotland, a loop of tartan cloth, draped loosely from the left side of the waist to the right shoulder, where the ends overlap and hang down. A jeweled clasp at the right shoulder holds it all in place. Short white gloves or lace mittens are also part of the ensemble. It would be awfully nice if these tartan loops could match the trews of the ladies' male partners, but that may be too much to ask for.

Tartan trews is exactly what the male guests (169, right) will be wearing, with harmonizing vests and fashionable tailcoats in velvet or cloth. In the case of the latter, the lapels are of satin, brocade, or velvet. White gloves are worn by all. A number of Highland-Dress alternatives are possible as coats: the 'Sheriff Muir' coat, which has side- and pocket-flaps, cuffs, and a stand-up collar. The 'Montrose Doublet,' which has a turn-down collar, is buttoned and without a vest. Instead a Dirk-Belt and Dirk (170, 171) are worn with it. All the Highland-Dress coats have metal buttons. Lace jabots, although no longer in fashion then, accessorize all Highland-Dress male costumes.

In *The Bride of Lammermoor* the author prescribes for Lucia's wedding-gown: white satin with Brussels lace, and a many-jeweled headdress. This is an odd statement, for in the 17th century where he places the action brides did not dress in white. That custom only developed after the French Revolution. However since the year is 1835, this Lucia shall wear 'white.' Judging from her appearance it is quite clear that 'her heart is not in it' and the look of her wedding-gown should support that feeling. If the fabric must be white satin, let it be at least the 'crepe-back' variety, which is both less shiny than regular satin and much softer in texture. Even 'off-white' may be preferable as color, because under stage-light a mass of white may be blinding, which is certainly not the impression Lucia should make. A few less petticoats than those worn by the other ladies may also be appropriate for this bride. A veil of lace, trimmed with a white flower-wreath, rather than one of tulle will also add to the sadness of her looks. Sir Walter's request for a jeweled headdress had better be forgotten, but her white gloves had better not. It would not be amiss if

TOP: Illus. 168; BOTTOM: Illus. 169.

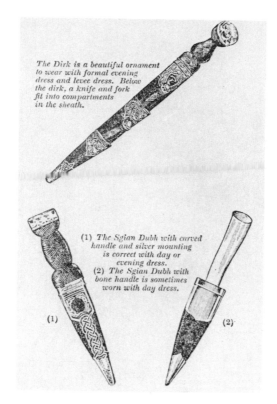

The Dirk is a beautiful ornament to wear with formal evening dress and levee dress. Below the dirk, a knife and fork fit into compartments in the sheath.

(1) The Sgian Dubh with carved handle and silver mounting is correct with day or evening dress.
(2) The Sgian Dubh with bone handle is sometimes worn with day dress.

(1)

(2)

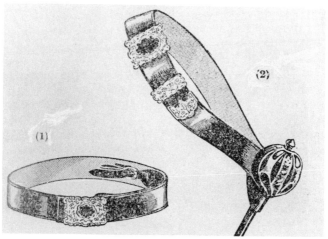

(2)

(1)

TOP: Illus. 170; BOTTOM: Illus. 171.

Illus. 172.

the guests whispered to each other: ''This is the saddest looking bride I have ever seen!'' (172)

Alisa now wears a dark dress similar to the one from Act I, but of a more 'dressy' fabric. There is still the collar and cap, but this time no apron and no gloves for this lady!

Although brides customarily dressed in white in the 1800's, there was no specific costume or color for bridegrooms. A pair of jolly trews of tartan cloth like that of the Ogilvy Clan would suit Arturo, while his fashionable velvet tailcoat and silk vest (173) might be chosen from two other colors in that Tartan. With his coat go the fashionable stock and white gloves. When Lucia and Arturo leave together after the wedding ceremony, they should look like an ill-matched couple.

Enrico wears for this occasion the same trews of the previous scene, but with a Dirk-Belted Monrose Doublet, which will enable him to carry a sword, come the confrontation with Edgardo. Lest he may be the only person who is armed (except for Normanno and the Guards), which would look as if he is anticipating a fight, it is a good idea if some of the male guests also wear Monrose Doublets with Dirks.

Edgardo arrives in travelling clothes, consisting of a dark grey Monrose Doublet with Belt and Dirk, trews and plaid in a Tartan of the Wallace Clan, a white stock, and a matching grey Balmoral Bonnet. Since he will have no occasion to change costumes after this, it must also be suitable for his appearance in the opera's final scene.

ACT 3   SCENE 1

Enrico has added a plaid and Balmoral Bonnet to his costume of the previous scene, while Edgardo has removed both plaid and Bonnet from his.

ACT 3   SCENE 2

'Cheerful dance-music can be heard from adjoining rooms,' states the libretto, which has prompted some producers to introduce ballet-dancers, not in 'adjoining rooms' but right on the stage. In such a case the ballerinas might wear tight-fitting tartan bodices, with full Balle-

Illus. 173.

rina-length skirts. In the hair they also wear a flower-wreath. The men wear matching tartan tights, and solid-colored vests over their Ballet shirts (174).

The introduction of such a ballet also implies the presence on stage of musicians. These can either be costumed in identical dark suits of the period, with contrasting vests, and white stocks, or they might don the uniforms of a Scottish Band. Yet, this might prove too colorful and therefore distracting.

Lucia enters dressed in a negligee (175). The historically correct garment of that period is not suitable in this situation. Possibly because of prevailing indoor temperatures those garments were made of sturdy fabrics. For the 'mad scene' Lucia requires a sheer ample negligee over a nightgown. The libretto describes her as 'dressed in a flowing white gown, her hair streams loosely over her shoulders.' This writer prefers pale grey over pale lavender for that purpose, but is in favor of the loose hair. A delicate matter to be considered are the blood stains on Lucia's garment and hands. It stands to reason that they are present, but have to be applied with great care and good taste or the effect may be counterproductive by evoking laughter.

ACT 3   SCENE 3

Edgardo repeats his costume from Act 2, Scene Two, but omits the plaid.

Raimondo wears again the black cape, beret and leggings of Act I, Scene One.

The male chorus in this scene is described in the libretto as 'a somber group.' The text indicates that Lucia is still alive until the death bell tolls. Therefore, they cannot be dressed in mourning, but must wear long, dark, hooded capes with black boots or boot-tops in order to produce the required 'somber' effect of the opera's 'finale.'

Illus. 174.

Illus. 175.

CHAPTER 8

LEHAR'S

Die lustige Witwe

Illus. 176

DIE LUSTIGE WITWE, *La Vedova Allegra, The Merry Widow, Den GladeEnke, LaVeuve Joyeuse, De vrolijke weduwe,* almost every country has adopted this operetta as its own. It has been performed in 15 different languages and eventually gained such worldwide popularity that a kind of 'Merry Widow' mania prevailed, to which a cartoon from the 1908 *Evening American* will attest (177). Even to this day a waist-cinching undergarment is referred to as a 'Merry Widow.' (178)

The Widow's inauspicious provenance is a matter of record. The intendants of Das Theater an der Wien in Vienna, where the operetta had its world premiere on December 28, 1905, were so convinced that they had a disaster on their hands, that they refused to spend any money on its production. Everything was dug out of 'the old trunks in the basement.' The Pontevedrian folk costumes in particular were not Pontevedrian at all (Pontevedria being an invented country in the first place), but Montenegran, much to the annoyance of the Montenegrans,

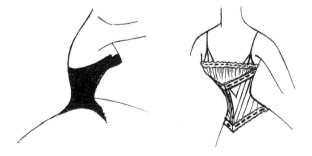

TOP: Illus. 177; BOTTOM: Illus. 178.

who proceeded to picket local productions on that account. The operetta became a huge success despite its modest production which may be a source of comfort to costumers who are forever expected to perform miracles on a limited budget. There is no doubt that 'The Merry Widow' should be a lavish-looking enterprise. It will strain the ingenuity of any costumer to have to achieve this with moderate means.

The time of action is given as 'the Present,' ergo 1905. In women's fashions that was the time of the 'straight front' silhouette (179), 'pigeon pouch' bodice, a tiny waist and curved spine with a consequently emphasized derriere. It is a silhouette that has a great deal of charm and is very typical of the period. In our practically corsetless times, one can only hope to emulate this silhouette with the help of a waist cincher (the aforementioned 'Merry Widow'), a boned bodice and a small bustle pad under the petticoat. It is well worth the effort.

ACT I

The operetta's first act takes place during a ball given at the Pontevedrian Embassy in Paris for the purpose of celebrating the birthday of that nation's Sovereign. It is a 'full dress' event; in other words, it is attended by all the high-ranking embassy personnel and their spouses, invited couples from foreign embassies in Paris, and other members of the Parisian 'haute monde.'

'Pontevedria' is the name of a fictitious Balkan country. In order to decide what kind of civilian and military clothes might have been worn by the natives of such a country, one can avail oneself of the rich folklore of the various nations that comprise this region. Members of the upper classes, however, would exclusively wear the fashionable clothes of the period.

The Pontevedrian male principal, Baron Mirka Zeta, the Ambassador, is a middle-aged gentleman. On this gala occasion he wears the full ambassadorial uniform, with medals and order-sash (180). Bogdanowitsch, the Embassy's military attaché, Kromow, its counselor, Pritschitsch, the elderly consul, and Njegus the Embassy secretary, all wear versions of the ambassadorial uniform, which differs from strictly military attire. It consists of an embroidered

TOP, LEFT: Illus. 179; BOTTOM, RIGHT: Illus. 180.

cutaway coat, vest, and long pants or knee breeches. All this may vary with the importance of the wearers' position and age. Of the Embassy's high-ranking personnel only Danilo Danilowitsch, its First Secretary, and incidentally, the operetta's leading man, is not in uniform. It was initially not his intention to attend the affair. Instead he was pursuing his favorite pastime: the Grisettes. When he enters he is wearing tails, a top hat, and evening coat (181). Furthermore, the status of the other male principals is not identified in the original libretto, although titles have been invented in later versions for two of them. Thus Vicomte Cascada became an Italian diplomat, Raoul de St. Brioche, a French ditto, while only Camille de Rossillon remains a tried-and-true civilian. All three would be properly attired in tail suits in this act, to which the diplomats might add some medals for the occasion. The male guests at this event would also be in tail suits of the period although a sprinkling of uniforms always helps to break the monotony and is furthermore entirely appropriate. 'Tail suits of the period' differ from modern ones in a generally tighter fit of coats, sleeves, and pants, hardly any shoulder padding, shorter tails, stand-up collars, and fairly small, straight bow ties (182). Vests were single-breasted and had points at the bottom. Footmen in lackey uniforms with possibly Pontevedrian touches, would naturally be in evidence at an Embassy ball.

Hanna Glawari, the Merry Widow, is the only female principal whose appearance in this act has been heralded in advance. Her 'entrance' must therefore be spectacular! (see Chapter-opening illustration, 176) She is in mourning for her recently deceased husband and is accordingly in black. But hers is not a modest little black dress. It should have plenty of glitter, can have a daring décolletage, although modestly veiled in sheer black, a sizable train, and a spectacular large-brimmed, plumed 'Merry Widow' hat. A black feather boa might not be out of place, nor black jet jewelry. Sheer black opera gloves will complete the picture. Needless to say, she is the only lady on stage totally in black.

Valencienne, Baron Zeta's young wife is the 'Zerlina' (Mozart: 'Don Giovanni') of this operetta, not as regards her social status, but because of her vacillating approach towards her flirtation with Camille de Rossillon. "I would and yet I wouldn't" seems to be both characters' theme song. The importance given in the operetta's plot to the ladies' possible infidelities and their husbands' reactions—which alternate between confidence, fears, hopes, despair, trust, and indigna-

TOP: Illus. 181; BOTTOM: Illus. 182.

tions in that regard—is rather typical of the prevailing Victorian morality. How different was the 18th-century attitude when infidelity was almost taken for granted!

Something a bit frilly seems in order for the charming Valencienne (183), with flowers in her hair and the inevitable white opera gloves, which are a must for all the female characters. Valencienne's mislaid fan, which plays such an important part in the plot, deserves some attention as well. Evidently it is small enough to fit into a man's inside breast pocket yet it must not be unobtrusive. Gold lace, highlighted with gold sequins, may be the answer.

Sylvane, the wife of Bogdanowitsch, and Olga (184), Kromow's better half, have received little character definition in the libretto. They are elegant young women, not shy of a little flirtation if the occasion arises. Any elegant evening gown that suits the wearer and fits the overall color scheme will do nicely for them, so long as they stand out in some way from the ladies of the ensemble, who should be a more anonymous group. A variety of feather or flower hair trimmings is also in order for all. The age of Praskowia, the wife of consul Pritschitsch, is referred to in the text. She is a bit older than the others and should be dressed accordingly (185), not only because people were more inclined to dress their age then, but because she makes a fool of herself in her sudden outburst of affection for Danilo.

A stage crowded with ladies in gowns with trains is always fraught with the possibilities of these trains being stepped on. To avoid such mishaps it has become the habit to attach a ribbon loop down the middle back of the skirt, which the wearers can place on their wrists, thereby keeping the trains out of danger's path. Alas, such a device was never used at the time. Most women's skirts had trains of one kind or another day and night and holding onto the skirt and picking it up in the middle-back was second nature to the ladies (186) and part of a girl's training as she reached the age of maturity, of which being old enough to wear a long skirt was an important part. Loops on skirts may be practical, but they are also entirely wrong.

ACT II

The second act takes place the following day in the garden of Mme. Glawari's mansion, since the lady has decided that it is now her

Illus. 183.

TOP, LEFT: Illus. 184; BOTTOM, RIGHT: Illus. 185.

Illus. 186.

turn to celebrate her Monarch's birthday. This feast is a strictly
Pontevedrian affair, however, and everyone is in native attire (187).
Even the guests from Parisian high society will attend in their versions
of Balkan-type folk dress, or else they would have to appear in a
second set of evening wear. Ladies of their class would under no
circumstances appear two nights in a row in the same dress. It is not a
problem. They have, after all, a choice among the best of Czech,
Yugoslavian, Bulgarian, Albanian, and Romanian folk costumes. Even
the members of the Embassy, Danilo included, should now be in
uniforms that demonstrate a strong Balkan influence. The libretto
states that the dancers are preceded upon their entrance by 'Guslars.'
(188) Intensive research has revealed that these are musicians who
play the 'Gusla,' a string instrument of Russian origin. Naturally, they
too are in native dress.

Hanna in her Pontevedrian costume (189) will render the famous
'Vilja' song and there can be no doubt that hers will be more splendid
than the others, including one of those flattering native headdresses.
Valencienne, Sylvane, Olga, and Praskowia must each aim to express
their own individuality in their native attire. Hanna's servants will also
be properly Pontevedrian in a modest way.

Boots for men and women are the accepted footwear to accessorize native Balkan costumes, which can pose a problem in a large
cast, especially for the ladies. Black hose, not too sheer, and black
pumps with a fairly low heel will be an acceptable alternative. If worst
comes to worst the gentlemen may have to be satisfied with boot tops,
although one should try to provide at least the male principals with
honest to goodness boots, so long as these are not 'Western' in style.

ACT III

"Later that evening" says the libretto, Mme. Glawari has her
garden transformed into a replica of Maxim's, a 'cafe chantant'
frequented by the haute- and demi-monde, where 'Grisettes' perform
the 'cancan.' It is one of Danilo's favorite hangouts. Logically this
arrangement makes no sense at all, for it implies that the entire cast of
the previous act will attend this party dressed in Pontevedrian costume, which seems hardly fitting. Most productions transfer this act
therefore to the actual Maxim locale. That way everybody has at least

Illus. 187.

Illus. 188.

Illus. 189.

a chance to go home and change. True, "it is going to be a long night!", yet it is entirely within the realm of possibilities. Changing the time to 'The following day' would make more sense still.

'Grisettes' were initially working girls who wore high necked, longskirted, very demure grey dresses and hats (190). ('Grisette' means: little grey one.) The cancan, which they danced in the coffee houses they frequented, consisted in part of kicking one leg very high up in the air, thereby revealing the inside of their petticoats, sheer black hose on garters, partly bare thighs, and panties. The dance originated in the middle of the 19th century, causing a sensation as well as a scandal. Police interference and protestations of moral indignation proved of no avail. Eventually 'Grisettes' became professional performers, while the cancan became a technically demanding dance with some acrobatic features. The costume too lost some of its demureness, but the long skirts, ruffled petticoats, gartered hose, bare thighs, panties, and also the hats remained. The temptation to substitute panty hose and short skirts should be resisted at all costs. The celebrated Martha Graham deserves our thanks for having demonstrated once and for all that it is entirely possible to dance in long skirts. Until that time dancers would insist that they could not dance in skirts that covered more than their thighs. Consequently cancan skirts, too, became shorter and shorter especially in America, thereby totally destroying the dance's essentially erotic character.

For reasons that are not entirely clear Valencienne has decided to join the Grisettes in this act. Her costume should therefore be exactly like theirs but of a different color. Evidently she performs the dance as if to the manner born, no mean feat for a singer. Assuming that this act also takes place in the evening, the visitors to Maxim's—male and female—would be in evening clothes, but not so formal as those worn at the embassy ball (191). For the ladies hats are absolutely essential (192) in such an environment while boas and other shoulder-covering accessories are also in order. There is plenty of evidence to prove that men too wore hats inside a cafe, but this is so against our present day sense of propriety that a concession can be made in that respect. All the embassy officials are now in evening attire, but occasional military uniforms are still a welcome variation. The messenger who delivers the telegram to the Ambassador can wear the embassy's footman's livery. It would be nice though if he had on top of that one of those long livery coats that were part of every footman's outdoor attire.

This chapter cannot be concluded without discussing Hanna's last

TOP, LEFT: Illus. 190; TOP, RIGHT: Illus. 191; BOTTOM: Illus. 192.

act costume. The lady has made it clear that she intends to marry Camille, which is an excellent reason for her to discard her widow's weeds. Incidentally, who will ever forget how this change was accomplished in the Lubitsch film, when suddenly everything that had been black before became white, not merely the clothes but all the furnishings as well, including even the lady's poodle. Alas, such movie magic is not available to us on the stage. The widow Glawari, soon to be Mme. de Rossillon, can now appear in a gorgeous white evening gown (193) of the period, complete with a feather hairdo of egrets and all the other suitable accessories. However, since her heart is not really in this liaison, it would be nice to postpone the transformation until it has become evident that she soon will be Mme. Danilowitsch instead. In that event she will at first wear another black dazzler, more suitable for a visit to Maxim's, preferably including a hat, and then change right on stage, something that can be accomplished with careful planning and rehearsing. If she is properly masked from the audience's view by a group of the other people on stage, and/or a screen which magically happens to be part of the stage furniture, or a few potted palms, this change can be effectively brought about. Even in this age of zippers and velcro such changes are tricky, but they can be successfully achieved and the effect on the audience is so stunning that it is in every sense worth the effort.

Illus. 193.

CHAPTER 9

TCHAIKOVSKY'S

The Queen of Spades

Illus. 194

T CHAIKOVSKY'S BROTHER MODESTE based the libretto for *The Queen of Spades* on Pushkin's short story of the same title. On one hand he expanded the events for theatrical purposes. The scene in the park, for instance, is wholly his invention. It has been suggested that the use of the children's chorus was based on the success of such a chorus in Bizet's *Carmen*. The brothers had seen the opera in Paris and admired it greatly. On the other hand, brother Modeste eliminated some salient parts of the story, not to the libretto's advantage. When, in the opera the Countess and Lisa see Herman for the first time they both exclaim: "Oh, my God, there is that man again!", or words to that effect. The facts are that the Countess has never set eyes on him before, while Lisa has observed him underneath her window for weeks and has even exchanged messages with him. Anyone who is involved in any way in the production of the opera is urged most strongly to read Pushkin's story. It will pay off in the end!

Establishing 'time' and 'place' is of the foremost importance when mounting a theatrical production. In the case of *The Queen of Spades* setting the place is no problem. It is evidently St. Petersburg, Russia from start to finish. Establishing the time of action is an entirely different matter. The only thing we know for certain is that the events occur during the reign of Tsarina Catherine II, who ruled from 1762 till 1796. At the closing of Act II, Scene 3, this lady almost puts in an appearance. 'Almost', because although her arrival is loudly proclaimed and heralded, the appearance on the stage of royalty was not within the realm of what was permissible then. Hence the curtain comes down just as she is about to make her entrance. The libretto states that 'The Countess,' one of the opera's leading characters, never abandoned the fashions of the 1770s (195), the time when she was known in Paris as "The Venus of Moscow" and when she had her liaison there with the Count St. Germain. Because the Countess is supposed to look grotesque in her 'ancien regime' elegance, it is important that what everyone else wears be as far removed from the styles of 1770 as possible. Since Catherine remained in good health until her sudden death in November 1796 (196), that year is the most likely choice for the time of the opera's action. In the nearly thirty years between the time of the Countess' Parisian adventures to that of the events portrayed in the opera, fashions had changed considerably. The difference in silhouette of the women's fashions from Rococo to Directoire (197) was especially significant, although it had not yet reached the extreme change occasioned by the 'Empire' fashions. Those who want to emphasize the contrast between the Countess' clothes versus those of all the other high-born ladies on stage, may want to cheat a little and advance the time to the early 1800s. In performance it is frequently done.

After the reign of Peter the Great foreign influence in Russia had gradually shifted from German and Dutch to French. Under Catherine II's rule the preference for everything French reached unknown heights. Everything *had* to be French, and if it were not, it pretended to be. Naturally such strong inclinations affected the clothes worn by the upper classes very strongly. Visually *The Queen of Spades* is well-nigh a French opera.

TOP: Illus. 195; BOTTOM: Illus. 196.

Illus. 197.

ACT I SCENE 1

The first scene of Act I takes place in the Summer Garden in St. Petersburg, on an early spring day. Aside from the principals, the libretto mentions those who frequent the park as: Little Girls, Nurse-maids, Governesses, Boys, a Boy-Captain, and Promenaders, consisting of: Young Ladies, Old Ladies, Young Beaux and Old Beaux (198). It would be nice if one could assume that on such a beautiful spring day people of all walks of life, old and young, rich and poor would gather in a public park to enjoy the end of a long winter, but such was not the case. People of the middle or lower classes did not participate in such frivolous pastimes. Contemporary lithographs (198) show people of the lower classes in these surroundings only as laborers or beggars. It is no coincidence that among those mentioned in the libretto only the nurse-maids and governesses are of the working class, and they are merely present to accompany and supervise the children of their upper-class employers (198).

The population of St. Petersburg, from middle class upward wore the same fashionable clothes as those worn throughout Europe. Children were dressed as miniature grown-ups in a modified way. The fabrics used for their clothes were lighter in weight and lighter of color. The boys who play soldier could add paper bicorns to their everyday wear, while the Boy-Captain might also add something resembling epaulettes, a sash and a wooden sword. Fortunately the promenaders of both sexes are divided into young and old categories. That presents the opportunity to display some costume variety, for there is no doubt that the older folks dressed far more conservatively than the younger ones both in fashion and in color. Older men (198) in particular adhered to wearing knee breeches long after those had been abandoned by the younger set in favor of ankle tights with boots or leggings, and somewhat later: long pants! Older ladies (198) would also cling to fashions of days gone by without going to extremes like the Countess by dressing 'ancien regime.'

Although in the entire opera only the principals Herman, Naru-mov, and Tomsky are cited in Pushkin's story as being of military rank, it is reasonable to assume that among the male promenaders there is a sprinkling of uniforms (199). Those among the young beaux would be on active duty and hence dressed in the latest military fashion with bicorns, ankle tights, and boots (200). Among the old

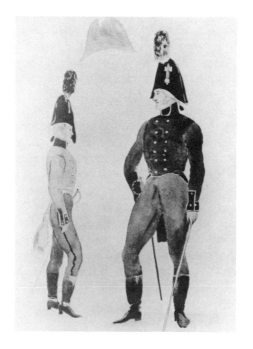

TOP: Illus. 198; BOTTOM: Illus. 199.

beaux one can expect to find some retired officers who cling to their uniforms of earlier days, complete with tricorns and knee breeches (201, 202).

It remains now to discover what nurse-maids (203) and governesses wore in St. Petersburg on an early spring day in 1796. Researchers will find to their dismay that, whereas there is plentiful information concerning native Russian costume reaching even to the far-flung corners of the Russian Empire, the attire of the common city dweller is totally ignored. Most likely it was not considered picturesque enough to deserve description. Since the ladies in question here are in the employ of upper-class families it can be expected that their clothes will be somewhat influenced by the taste of their employers. A full, longsleeved high-necked blouse would be worn under that Russian institution the 'Sarafan,' a smock-like sleeveless full-length garment. Babushka-like headcoverings are in order. These can vary, depending on whether they are tied right over the hair, or whether there is a cap underneath, which at times had a point in front. Light grey and light blue seem appropriate colors for the nurse-maids' Sarafans, accompanied with white aprons and white babushkas. The governesses (204) are a bit more formidable. The colors of their skirts and longsleeved peplumed bodices are darker, as are their complementary aprons and headdresses.

The principals in Act I, Scene 1 are, in order of appearance, Tchekalinsky (205) and Sourin (206), both young men and gambling companions of Herman, the opera's leading man, whose behavior they study and discuss. Very little is revealed of their individual character, but they are not beyond teasing Herman about his gambling obsession and playing pranks on him in that respect. They both wear fashionable suits of the period without being dandies. This is best expressed by the modesty of their neckwear, which at that time could be extreme, consisting as it did of high collars, which often concealed the chin, elaborately draped neck scarves, which did the same, and profusely ruffled shirt fronts. In the colors of their suits one should attempt to make them stand out from the crowd. Naturally they would not be outdoors without accompanying headgear. Herman is an officer of the Corps of Engineers and hence he is in uniform. This Corps does not rank high among the military and Herman's dark green uniform coat is a simple one, with shoulderboards in lieu of epaulettes. Although the ankle tights accompanying the coat are usually white or off-white, in Herman's case they should match the coat, thereby underlining the

TOP: Illus. 200; BOTTOM, LEFT: Illus. 201; BOTTOM, RIGHT: Illus.
202.

TOP: Illus. 203; BOTTOM: Illus. 204.

Illus. 205.

Illus. 206.

character's prevailing somber mood, making him different from the others and flattering his girth. According to Pushkin, Herman's uniform has a beaver collar and a matching beaver shako. Naturally he wears boots, which are invariably black for the military. Civilians would ocasionally indulge in the wearing of brown boots. Herman's friend Count Tomsky (207) is a rather jolly fellow. It is he who sings the Ballad of the Countess' Paris adventures and in the last act also regales his gambling companions with a merry ditty. The reason he possesses such intimate details about the Countess' life stems no doubt from the fact that in Pushkin's story he is that lady's grandson. As was mentioned earlier, Pushkin refers to him as "a young officer." In the story's last sentence he is promoted to the rank of captain. Under these circumstances it is suggested that in the opera he be in Hussar's uniform with epaulettes and all the braid and aiguilettes such a uniform demands. Prince Yeletsky, Lisa's hapless fiancé, wears an elegant daytime suit of the period, complete with boots and bicorn (208). Being a Prince and a bridegroom to be, he might add a cape to his suit or wear a redingote instead of a frockcoat.

The opera's librettist has upgraded Lisa from being merely the Countess' penniless ward to being her granddaughter, without improving her sad disposition however. Throughout the opera she has very few happy moments, which certainly must be reflected in the clothes she wears. In Act I this should be an elegant Directoire ensemble and bonnet of a subdued color and soft fabric (see chapter-opening illustration, 194).

As was mentioned earlier, the Countess has chosen to adhere to the fashions of 1770 when she was the belle of Parisian gambling establishments. In addition to dressing 'ancien regime' she now also gives the impression of a 'scarecrow.' Leaning on a cane as she does, she comes across in her 1770 walking dress as a caricature (209), although an imposing one. The realization of these characteristics via her costumes must come about through a mixture of unlikely fabrics and the manner in which the gown is decorated and trimmed to create a somewhat ghost-like impression. Her equally outdated high wig and headdress must also be not merely old fashioned, but slightly peculiar as well, which will help greatly to achieve the desired effect. Naturally her make-up is also of great importance. She should look every bit her 82 years of age, but in addition her pale cheeks are overly rouged and covered with beauty marks.

TOP, LEFT: Illus. 207; TOP, RIGHT: Illus. 208; BOTTOM: Illus. 209.

SCENE 2

The scene in Lisa's room presents a romantic gathering of Lisa, her close friend Pauline and a group of other friends. It has the air of a nostalgic, female bachelor's party. Lisa is sad throughout this scene and Pauline's song does not help to cheer things up. Only her final Russian song in which the other girls join has a more joyful air. For this occasion everybody wears elegant, high-waisted afternoon gowns of Directoire fashion. Lisa's is subdued in color (210), Pauline's of a lighter, harmonizing one, the others (211) in assorted pastel shades. Small headdresses often of turban-like genre were also in vogue with Directoire gowns. The Governess (212) who comes in to break up the party is either French or strongly French influenced. Her Directoire gown is dark, longsleeved, with a ruffle around the neck, a long narrow apron, and a severe lace headdress. Lisa's servant Mascha, who comes to extinguish the lights after the guests have left, is dressed in a Sarafan, blouse, apron and babushka, like the other servants in Act I (213). When Herman enters Lisa's room via the balcony he may have added a cape to his uniform. On one hand this could help to hide his identity, but on the other it might impair his mobility.

The Schirmer Edition of the opera's piano vocal score states that the Countess, with some servants, now enters Lisa's room "dressed in night attire," which is an error. The Russian score mentions that she is "fully clothed" which does not make any sense either from a theatrical point of view. If the Countess in a fit of annoyance at the noise emanating from Lisa's room would have stormed out in her nightgown, one of her servants would no doubt hastily have put a robe over it for the sake of decorum alone. That she would have remained "fully clothed" in her cumbersome paniered dress is equally unlikely. First of all, quite some time had elapsed since she returned from her walk in the park. Secondly, because 18th-century dress-up clothes were so involved, what with wigs for both sexes and unwieldy paniers for the ladies, both genders remained in elegant 'undress' as long as possible and reverted back to it as soon as possible. It even became fashionable to have one's portrait painted thusly undressed. The Countess can therefore be expected to have worn one of those voluminous 'robes volantes' that were fashionable for elegant undress, accompanied with an equally voluminous lace cap over her closely

TOP: Illus. 210; BOTTOM: Illus. 211.

Illus. 212.

Illus. 213.

cropped hair (214). The servants' clothes will be discussed in some more detail in a later scene, when these ladies play an important part.

ACT II   SCENE 1

Masked balls were popular in the 18th and 19th centuries, and because they present the opportunity to display characters in disguise they are a welcome device in theatrical productions, operas included (215, 216, 217, 218). As everyone knows, the title of one famous opera is: *Un Ballo in Maschera,* and some of the observations regarding such festivities are of necessity repeated in the chapter devoted to that opera. In the 19th century it became popular to choose a theme for such occasions, but in earlier days it was a free-for-all. 'Commedia dell'arte' characters remained favorites as well as interpretations of oriental Potentates. From Mozart's *Cosi fan tutte* we recall that Despina's disguises as a Doctor and a Notary are referred to as 'masquerades.' For those who wanted the easy way out 'dominos' (basically 'monk's habits') were a suitable and legitimate cover-all, while masks were a *must* regardless of the choice of costume. Such variable options in the choice of costume are exceedingly advantageous to the costumer, who can use this diversity for the purpose of characterization.

The masked ball in question takes place at the home of a rich dignitary and is, as was not uncommon, a multifaceted festivity, with guests strolling in and out to observe alternately fireworks and the performance of a 'Pastoral.' It will all culminate in the arrival of the Tsarina and her retinue. All these events are announced to the guests by a Master of Ceremonies (219), who wears a lackey's uniform that hails from the times of Louis XIV and hence consists of a 'justaucorps' coat, long vest, knee breeches, jabot, shoulder sash, buckled shoes and a shoulder-length wig. Other lackeys (220) are costumed one Louis later, Louis XV to be exact, while those who set the stage for the upcoming Pastoral will wear shirts, vests, and breeches more of the workman's genre.

The score mentions a 'choir of singers on a platform,' whose sole function exists in singing a 'Welcome!' chorus to the guests. They will most likely sing the choral parts in the ensuing Pastoral for which occasion they will be dressed as 18th-century shepherds and shepherd-

Illus. 214.

TOP: Illus. 215; BOTTOM: Illus. 216.

Illus. 217.

Illus. 218.

TOP: Illus. 219; BOTTOM: Illus. 220.

esses. To reveal these costumes prematurely would be a mistake. An effective and relatively inexpensive solution to this problem would be to superimpose on the Pastoral costumes a set of colorful organza dominos. Tchekalinsky and Sourin take the part in this scene of fleeting figures who, in passing, whisper bewildering messages to Herman. Dark-hued dominos in shiny fabrics seem appropriate for that purpose. Tomsky, who will soon interpret the part of Pluto in the Pastoral should overdress in a brightly-colored, possibly figured domino. The scene and aria of Yeletsky and Lisa that follow are strangely reminiscent of the relationship between Pasha Selim and Konstanze in Mozart's *Entfüehrung*. Therefore a Turkish nobleman's robes and turban are appropriate for Yeletsky (221), while a stylishly veiled Sultana's costume would suit Lisa (222). For Herman the elegant Harlequin costume of a rejected lover seems relevant (223). It is significant that the score mentions that Herman does not wear a mask, which is definitely an exception to the rule. Without masks it would not be a 'Bal Masque.'

'Pastorales' were a popular 17th-century form of theatrical entertainment and one of the forerunners of opera. In the 18th century especially they were extravagantly costumed without much regard to the protagonists' humble status. On this occasion historical accuracy need not be adhered to too strictly in that respect. Without emulating Mme. Favart, who interpreted the role of the shepherdess Bastienne in authentic costume, wooden shoes and all, pleasingly stylized versions of 18th-century shepherds and shepherdesses will suit this entertainment. Of the leading characters Daphnis (224, left) and Chloe (224, right), Lisa's friend Pauline is cast in the role of Daphnis. It is important, therefore, that this lady have the physical attributes which will transform her into an acceptable 'Cherubino-type' figure. Tomsky, as Pluto (225), should wear the theatrically popular 18th-century interpretation of a Roman general, with a plumed helmet and a sizable cape-like drapery. His attendants wear very modified versions of that style of costume.

It is entirely in keeping with her character that the Countess' only adherence to the rules of the ball consists in the wearing of a mask, which she may carry on a stick in her hand. Otherwise she wears an extravagantly overdone, widely paniered court gown and high powdered wig, bedecked with plumes (226).

Of the much heralded and vocally acclaimed entrance of Tsarina

TOP, LEFT: Illus. 221; BOTTOM, RIGHT: Illus. 222.

TOP: Illus. 223; BOTTOM: Illus. 224.

Illus. 225.

Catherine II the audience beholds merely some members of her retinue consisting of four pages, clad in semi-Russian style page costumes (227).

ACT II   SCENE 2

Upon entering the Countess' bedroom Herman is again in uniform. If he had not already donned a cape in the 'balcony scene' he should definitely wear one now.

From the music sung by the Countess' maids (228) and servants (229) it is clear that they are a lot of old biddies who have maternal feelings towards their mistress. Their music is all but a lullaby. Accordingly they wear assorted dark skirts over petticoats. The tops are of matching fabric or slightly different, long sleeved and with a peplum. They all have aprons and babushkas, in dark, harmonizing colors. Some may have additional shoulder scarves.

Lisa could repeat her dress from the 'balcony scene' with an added scarf, or with that scarf she may wear another similar gown.

The Countess (230) in her nightgown makes a quite different impression than she did in her 'ancien regime' robes. Without the rouge and the beauty spots, the paniers and the powdered wig, the grotesque aspects have disappeared. She is now a frail, very old lady, dressed in a nightgown of pale grey sheer fabric over pale lavender crepe-back satin. A somewhat ghost-like effect may be created by spraying the fabric and adding some pieces of darker grey sheer in several places. The lace headdress over her close cropped white hair is still substantial but again not grotesque. In this frail and tired condition she sings the air from Grétry's opera *Richard Coeur de Lion,* and it is in this condition that Herman scares her to death.

ACT III   SCENE 1

In the barracks scene Herman is in his shirtsleeves, his dark green ankle tights and boots (231). One assumes that the 'Ghost of the Countess' is a projection, resembling in a ghostly manner how she looked in the previous scene.

TOP, LEFT: Illus. 226; BOTTOM, RIGHT: Illus. 227.

TOP: Illus. 228; BOTTOM: Illus. 229.

Illus. 230.

SCENE 2
(A canal near the Winter Palace.)

Lisa (232), in mourning because of the death of her grandmother, wears a simple but fashionable winter-outdoor ensemble of the period, with a matching sheer head scarf. Herman is again in full uniform, with cape, shako, and boots.

SCENE 3

The final scene takes place in a gambling establishment owned by Tchaplitsky (233), who participates in the game. Besides the assorted gambling participants, Tomsky, Tchekalinsky, Sourin, and Namourov are present, and a little later Prince Yeletsky as well. Namourov is an officer in the Horse Guards, Pushkin tells us, hence he is in Hussar's uniform, and a few other guests may be in uniform as well. Yeletsky, in mourning because of Lisa's death, is entirely in black. All the others wear fashionable suits of the period (234), some with frock coats, some with redingotes. Hats were commonly worn indoors in such an establishment. They consist mostly of bicorns, but for the first time top hats, in the shape peculiar to the period, started their long career through the history of men's fashions.

Waiters wear Russian shirts, full black pants tucked into black boots, and half aprons.

As a final footnote it may not be amiss to recall here this writer's personal involvement in costuming *The Queen of Spades* for a production that took place in the Berkshire Music Center in 1951. Although the score indicates that the Countess retires to her boudoir to change from her ball dress into her night attire, the stage in Tanglewood would not accommodate a 'boudoir.' Therefore, the change had to be accomplished in full view of the audience, a hazardous undertaking at best. It was successfully accomplished, however, in the following manner: The Countess underdressed her nightgown under the ballgown. The latter was not closed in the back but held together there by yours truly, who shaved off his mustache for the occasion and dressed like one of the servants, babushka and all. When he let go of the Countess' gown it fell to the floor and she, somewhat concealed by the surrounding servants, carefully stepped out of it. The pseudo

TOP, LEFT: Illus. 231; BOTTOM, RIGHT: Illus. 232.

Illus. 233.

Illus. 234.

servant then proceeded to remove the wig and replace it with a night cap he carried in a pocket in his skirt. Then, after wiping the excess rouge and beauty spots from the Countess' face, the deed was accomplished. Transformations of this kind can be successful if they are carefully rehearsed and they wlll strike the audience as sheer magic.

CHAPTER *10*

VERDI'S

Rigoletto

Illus. 235

*T*HE CENSOR WHO CAUSED Verdi and his librettists such grief in the case of *Un Ballo in Maschera* actually did them a favor in respect to *Rigoletto*. King Francis I, 'Le Grand Roi Francois' as he was called was in every respect an 'Absolute King.' In the early to middle 16th century, when he reigned, a wholly different moral code prevailed for such a person than in 1832 when Victor Hugo wrote *Le Roi S'Amuse,* or in 1851, when Piave wrote the libretto for *La Maledizione* which was based on Hugo's play. To give an example of the changing morality through the ages: Francis' mother Louise deSavoie and his sister Marguerite de Navarre, both deeply religious women, were in the habit of supplying their son and brother with mistresses, while in 1936 the King of England had to abdicate in order to be able to marry a divorcee. Considering that Hugo's play was initially banned by the censor as well, Verdi and Piave might have seen the handwriting on the wall. It is ultimately safer to blame a libertine little Duke of Mantua for his flagrant profligacies, than a famous historical character, who was supposed to behave that way in the first place. Piave followed Hugo's play closely, omitting only the last act's final scene in which the populace, aroused by Rigoletto's cries, arrive on the scene. A surgeon among them established that Sparafucile's knife was not the cause of Gilda's death, but rather the tight hold Rigoletto had on her which caused her lungs to fill with blood, adding insult to injury, one might say.

In the process of transferring the opera's locale, title and names, the period was advanced for unknown reasons to the century's third quarter. Especially regarding men's fashions, that change was not inconsiderable, actually a modification, which this writer for one welcomes. Francis I of France and Henry VIII of England who were great adversaries, nevertheless wore the same fashions of their time, which happened to suit both personalities. The male styles of their successors with which one identifies Phillip II of Spain, the Huguenot de Coligny brothers, or the Duke of Essex, to mention but a few, are more suitable for the *Rigoletto* nobility (236).

ACT I   SCENE 1

Although Count Monterone refers to the Duke's gatherings as orgies, Verdi's music belies that notion. The libretto describes the participants of the opening scene as 'a crowd of noblemen and ladies, elegantly attired.' (237) Of the men that excludes only Rigoletto, Count Monterone, two halberdiers, pages, and servants. All the others wear versions of the mid 16th-century styles consisting of 'doublets,' frequently with a pointed waistline and peplum flaps. Underneath the doublet an elegant shirt was worn which had a pleated ruffle at the collar and the wrists. The fabric of the doublet was frequently slashed to reveal the shirt underneath. The same was true of the sleeves which often had some fullness at the shoulder or wings. If the sleeves were fuller they would be paned or slashed, again revealing the shirt sleeve underneath. This also applied to the puffed trunk-hose, which covered the hips and thighs. Tights or long hose would cover the rest of the legs except in the case of 'canions' which covered the thigh to just below the knee. In that event the hose halted just above the knee. The diligent researcher will find many variations of this type of costume,

TOP: Illus. 236; BOTTOM: Illus. 237.

which helps in giving individual characters their own personality. Despite all the variations all men's costumes had one feature in common: the 'codpiece.' It was in fact the last time in the history of Western men's fashions that the existence of male genitalia was acknowledged in dress. At that particular time the codpiece had even become a fashion item. Frequently of a contrasting color from the trunk-hose, it was at times slashed, embroidered, bejewelled and. . . . stuffed! While in present-day productions of the opera the codpiece is usually omitted, some stage-directors might want to avail themselves of this curious costume detail for purposes of characterization!

Shoulder capes in splendid fabrics, frequently fur trimmed and with hanging sleeves, must be part of each courtiers' costume, no less than a choice of the variety of hats that were fashionable then. They were often trimmed with feathers and jewels. Jeweled necklaces were not uncommon either. Swords, which would be brandished at the slightest provocation were also part of the courtiers' attire. Tied around the waist with a belt, they were frequently studded with jewels.

'Ruffs,' (238) a popular fashion item at the time for men and women, have purposely not been mentioned here. In order to look right they must fit snugly around the throat, something all singers rightly abhor. The shirt's neck ruffle, pleated like a ruff and attached to the doublet's collar, will furnish a suitable and welcome substitute.

Naturally all the costumes must be color-coordinated, but choosing the same color for all of them is a mistake. This is not a chorus line.

Among all the elegantly attired gentlemen in this scene the Duke must be the most elegant of them all (239). To usurp some of the colors of royalty might not be amiss for this purpose. A doublet and trunk-hose of gold brocade, decorated with gold braided bandings and jewels might just be the thing for him as well as an armhole cape of royal velvet, trimmed with ermine.

The libretto does not mention Count Ceprano's weight problem, but in the play he is referred to as "one of the fattest men in France." (240) The idea has merit and one should not hesitate to pad Ceprano's figure into obesity. Foam rubber is recommended for this purpose. It is also helpful to the plot if color- and style-wise Count and Countess Ceprano seem an ill-matched couple.

The old Count Monterone should be costumed 'ancien regime.' (241, 242) A three-quarters length black tunic is worn under a long black, fur trimmed armhole cloak of rich fabric, as becomes a

TOP: Illus. 238; BOTTOM, LEFT: Illus. 239; BOTTOM, RIGHT: Illus. 240.

nobleman. Black hose, black shoes, and a black hat complete his costume. The starkness of his appearance indicates he represents 'conscience' and 'retribution.'

Of the other male principals Borsa (243) seems to be the Duke's confidant, as the scene's opening conversation indicates, while Rigoletto refers to Marullo (244) as "kind of heart and spirit," characteristics of which conscientious costumers will avail themselves. Rigoletto is a hunchbacked dwarf (chapter-opening illustration, 235), a combination of two conditions. The first was caused most likely by a birth accident—or by an accident during the mother's pregnancy—while the other may be a hormone deficiency. (Being a dwarf was so profitable then that parents stunted their children's growth by keeping them confined in cubicles.) With the advance of medicine the first condition is usually preventable, while the second one is sometimes curable. This is cause for much rejoicing except on the part of the costumer who is faced with the task of transforming a strapping six-foot baritone into a misshapen dwarf. Optical illusion has its decided limitations and despite all the tricks of the trade it can only make a tall person seem shorter so long as he is alone on the stage. No sooner does he stand next to a 5'3" Gilda, or a 5'10" Duke, then his real height will be evident, unless he stands in a hole or they wear platform shoes. In the opera there are 14 references to Rigoletto's condition (which includes calling him: Buffoon!), so there is no possibility of ignoring the matter. Luckily the traditional court-jester's costume is helpful in this respect. Based on the Burgundian mi-parti fashions of the 15th century it tends to cut the body up horizontally, vertically and diagonally. It was trimmed with many bells known as 'folly bells.' These were a fashionable costume decoration for men and women in the 15th-century Burgundian styles and persisted in the court-jester's costume. Usually a scalloped shoulder cape, with a tight-fitting hood, boasting asses' ears, were part of the jester's costume. In his hand he carried a scepter, the so called 'Marotte' which was in turn topped by a fool's head, complete with asses' ears, etc. And there were bells everywhere. In the opera those bells had better be soundless.

Naturally, a 'hunchback' requires a hunch, which must be a specially constructed undergarment over which the fool's costume is carefully fitted. Merely two shoulder-pads sewn to a T shirt in the region of the shoulderblade will not do the trick. Its protrusion, which the hunch represents, is often accompanied by one raised shoulder on

TOP: Illus. 241; BOTTOM; Illus. 242.

Illus. 243.

Illus. 244.

the same side, something padding will accomplish, while the effect of the twisted spine can be achieved by padding the opposite hip. A lift under one foot will furthermore produce a limp. Rigoletto refers to himself as 'an old man' and one imagines a hunchback's face as being emaciated, with a hooked nose and sharp chin. Clever make-up will accomplish that. However, no amount of craftsmanship can achieve the desired result unless the performer adopts the stance, walk, demeanor, nay the 'soul' of the character he is portraying.

Military uniforms as we know them did not exist until the 18th century. Similarity of cut and color, the bearing of heraldic emblems and the donning of part to full armor, were used to represent military attire. Accordingly, the halberdiers (245) that lead away Monterone should wear identical cloth suits of the period, possibly with helmets, breast-plates, and of course: halberds. The servants are costumed in identical cloth costumes. A mi-parti division of the doublets in the Duke's colors is suggested. Pages' (246) costumes were no different from anyone else's either. Here again the application of the identical color and cut (if there are more than one) will achieve a 'uniform' look.

The role of the Courtiers, male and female, is a curious one in this scene. The libretto mentions them at first as "moving through the inner rooms," some time later as "crossing the room," (whereupon the Duke reflects on the ladies' beauty) and once again at the Countess Ceprano's entrance. After that the ladies seem to drift off (in order to powder their noses no doubt) while the male Courtiers remain on stage and join in the action, also vocally. At the 'Tutto e Festa' chorus "a crowd of dancers invades the room" states the libretto. Evidently the ladies have returned to join their husbands in a courtly dance. Since these ladies never sing they might as well be dancers, thereby inducing the singing Courtiers to put their best foot forward as well.

After the Duke exits with the Countess Ceprano, followed by her angry husband, and Rigoletto muses on the Duke's ability to find pleasure in women wherever he goes, the score, but not the libretto, states: "Meantime the Perigordino (initially a French folk-dance) is danced on the stage." This dance is of a very different nature than the courtly "Tutto e Festa" one and suggests that it is performed by hired entertainers like Saltimbanques, tumblers (247), and acrobats. This would lend their costumes a more gypsy-like air, as depicted in the etchings of Jacques Callot (although these are of a somewhat later vintage).

TOP, LEFT: Illus. 245; BOTTOM, RIGHT: Illus. 246.

The ladies in *Rigoletto*'s opening scene play (see 237) decidedly second fiddle in every respect except visually. The vocal utterances of the Countess Ceprano (248), the only woman who sings in this scene, are restricted to three lines. Her vocal range is equally limited. Obviously this lady may be cast primarily for her looks and figure. A brocaded gown in a shade which complements the Duke, but not necessarily her husband's, is worn over a modest farthingale. Tight sleeves with a shoulder puff are richly ornamented. The gown has a daring décolleté, possibly modified by a sheer Medici collar, edged in a gold lace ruffle. A jeweled headdress and multiple necklaces should cause this lady to "outshine the many beauties at this event" as the libretto states. Many of the gowns of this period sported high necklines and it may be a good idea to let the Countess Ceprano be the only lady with some skin exposure. To create a set of attractive gowns of that period which will complement the courtiers' costumes should not be too difficult a task.

ACT I   SCENE 2

Rigoletto's civilian costume (249) is in total contrast to his professional one. Although the jester's attire has its gaudy aspects it is not cheap, but in every respect up to the Duke's court standards. His personal clothes are entirely in keeping with the other side of his character: dark and unobtrusive. They consist of a loose, knee-length tunic of a dark blue-green cloth (the color merely the writer's preference), a hooded shoulder-collar, and a leather belt. The tunic is not cut to allow for the hunch and therefore hikes up on one side. Complementary tights, slippers, and a large cape complete his costume. There are several references to men "wrapping themselves in their capes," Rigoletto included. Most likely that means that they grabbed the bottom right hand corner of the cape and threw it over their left shoulder. Later on in this scene, when he unwittingly participates in the abduction of Gilda, he wears a mask and is blindfolded. Evidently the night was so dark that Rigoletto was unaware of being blindfolded. On the stage it is a little difficult to create such darkness, yet it is terribly important because the opera's entire plot hinges on it.

Sparafucile is a 'bravo,' (250) a hired assassin, a gypsy and a Burgundian to boot. The reference to Burgundy has no further charac-

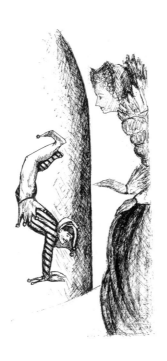

TOP: Illus. 247; BOTTOM, LEFT: Illus. 248; BOTTOM, RIGHT: Illus. 249.

ter significance. In the original French play the word Bourgognon was used as a rhyme word and somehow it stuck. Sparafucile is a sinister crook with a certain dash, who also has his own code of honor regarding his clients and proves to be a soft touch for his sister Maddalena's pleading. Consequently, he looks just right in a combination of brown and black leather for his much slashed doublet and trunk-hose. A pair of hip boots would suit his character and he too wraps himself in a large black cloak.

In the play Rigoletto refers to Gilda's hair as dark, but in view of her enduring innocence and as an opposite to Maddalena, who as a gypsy can only have black tresses, Gilda had better be a blond (251). Her dress of a lightweight, light colored non-silk fabric, is of a simple but flattering cut, trimmed with bands of a darker velvet, like the maidens depicted in Holbein's paintings. Although very little time elapses between the Duke's departure and the moment of her abduction, it is better to assume that she had retired for the night and is now in the 16th-century equivalent of a nightgown. It would be a white (or off-white) lightweight, loose-fitting garment, carefully tailored or gathered under the bust in order to flatter the figure. After all she will be seen in that nightgown throughout the second act, in a somewhat disheveled state to be sure, but not unattractive. The scarf which Rigoletto finds and recognizes may be assumed to have been part of that costume.

Giovanna is a middle-aged matron-housekeeper, clad in a dark cloth, possibly grey, gown with white accessories and headdress of the period. She may wear a long apron and from her waist hangs a purse (wherein to put the Duke's money) and a chatelaine (252).

The Duke, now Gualtier Malde, wears the simple woolen doublet and trunk hose, with an armhole cloak and hat of an impecunious student (253). Despite its simplicity it must be an attractive costume, though startlingly different from the Duke's festive costume of the previous scene. The color of his costume must complement Gilda's in order to present a harmonious couple.

It is interesting to observe that this impecunious student can afford to bribe Giovanna without arousing her suspicion.

All the courtiers have 'wrapped themselves' in large capes of varying dark hues (254, 255), which they put on top of whatever they may be wearing underneath. This situation will be discussed at some length in the following act. One matter not open for discussion is that they all require masks in this scene and that they are armed. The oval

Illus. 250.

TOP, LEFT: Illus. 251; BOTTOM, RIGHT: Illus. 252.

Illus. 253.

masks usually seen in that period may need some special adjustment in order not to interfere with the abductors' vocalism.

ACT II

The morning after Gilda's abduction the Duke appears from his bedroom in a brocaded 16th-century dressing gown on top of whatever he wears in bed, if anything (256).

The courtiers are now no longer in their 'party attire' of the previous evening, but in whatever the well-dressed courtier wears during the day. If such a drastic change of costumes for a large part of the cast proves more than the traffic can bear, we may have to settle for repeating the costumes of the previous evening, but stripped of shoulder capes, armhole cloaks, hats and whatever else was added to the basic costume to make it more festive, including reluctantly, even the swords.

Rigoletto is again in his jester's costume, Gilda in her nightgown. Monterone, the page, the guards and the footman all repeat their Act I costumes.

ACT III

Rigoletto repeats his civilian costume. Gilda wears a long hooded cape to complement her Act I, Scene 2 gown. Sparafucile now inside the house, has removed his leather doublet revealing the rough homespun shirt he wore underneath it. The Duke is supposed to wear a ''simple cavalry uniform.'' (257) As was pointed out earlier, military uniforms did not exist in the 16th century. A civilian suit with a 'military air,' boots included, will have to suffice. Adding a helmet and a metal breastplate may add to the military feeling. Since obviously a shouldercape is part of such an outfit the back part of the armor can be omitted. In preparation of things to come the Duke may relieve himself of these items in his upstairs bedroom.

It is not so easy to ascertain what a 16th-century gypsy may have worn, but of one thing we can be certain: it was seductive! Seductiveness has been the operatic gypsy's stock in trade be she Bizet's 'Carmen,' Verdi's 'Maddalena,' (258) or Rossini's 'Zaida' (*Il Turco in Italia*). An off-the-shoulder peasant blouse, a bright-laced bodice with

TOP, LEFT: Illus. 254; BOTTOM, RIGHT: Illus. 255.

Illus. 256.

Illus. 257.

waist tabs for a 16th-century touch, a full calf-length skirt tucked up over a striped second skirt and a scarf in her hair, bare legs and (the condition of the stage floor permitting) bare feet, and here is a gypsy no Duke will be able to resist.

For Gilda's final appearance she wears the men's clothes (259) Rigoletto had prepared for her at their home. It consists of a dark cloth doublet, matching trunk-hose, boots with spurs, a hat, and a shoulder cape. It is in this costume that Gilda makes the ultimate sacrifice.

TOP, LEFT: Illus. 258; BOTTOM, RIGHT: Illus. 259.

CHAPTER *11*

PUCCINI'S

La Rondine

Illus. 260

*C*OMPOSERS WHO CONTEMPLATE creating an opera frequently think in terms of a story with a contemporary plot. Producers who invest their money in such an enterprise are inclined to prefer historical settings for the new opus: something that will hurt no one's feelings. It was thus with Verdi's *La Traviata,* which, against the composer's specific wishes, was set in the time of King Louis XIV for its world premiere in 1853, a difference of almost 150 years. From the outset Puccini thought of *La Rondine* as a contemporary story, but on opening night the setting proved to be: Second Empire, in the eighteen sixties. The difference of a mere 55 years was now considered sufficient to soothe the producer's nerves. In both cases it was found impossible to acknowledge the present day existence of a social phenomenon: the Demimonde Courtesan, or, to put it more bluntly: ''a kept woman.'' So much for Victorian morality.

From a costumer's point of view the year 1914 is also problematic as a setting for the opera, but for a very different reason. The opera's second act, at the Bal Bullier, contains a great deal of waltz music, to which those in attendance are expected to dance. If we no longer have to worry about a great mass of crinolines bumping into each other, the ladies' fashions of 1914 do not lend themselves to graceful waltzing either (261). Its skirts were straight and narrow, with occasional touches of the preceding 'hobble-skirt' fashions. Going back a few years between 1905 and 1909 solves that problem, and it is the time suggested for *La Rondine* (chapter-opening illustration, 260).

ACT I

When the curtain rises Magda de Civry, the mistress of Rambaldo Fernandez, is hostess at a dinner party in her apartment. Since dinner is over, she is now serving coffee, assisted by her maid Lisette. Being a hostess, Magda is appropriately clad in an elegant 'hostess gown.' (262) This gown has a slight negligee touch to it, consisting as it does of a décolleté, sleeveless gown under a harmonizing loose, sheer, long-sleeved coat. This does not only differentiate her from the other female guests, but aids in her later, spectacular transformation. Magda's friends who attend the party are Yvette, Bianca, and Suzy. They are lighthearted young women of Magda's genre. Their sense of humor must reflect in the elegant afternoon gowns (263) they wear, each in keeping with their own personalities.

Lisette is Magda's maid (264), whose close ties to her mistress permit her to speak more freely than one usually expects from a girl of her station. Instead of the standard maid's uniform, she wears a light colored longsleeved blouse with a somewhat darker skirt, to which a ruffled bib-apron and maid's cap are added.

Of the male characters in this act, Rambaldo, Magda's wealthy patron (265), may be assumed to be a bit older than the other men. He wears a dark grey Prince Albert coat with lighter grey pants and double-breasted vest. A wing collar and Ascot tie complete his costume, which boasts in addition an expensive, but not ostentatious, tie pin, watch fob, and rings. His friends, Perichaud, Gobin, and Crebillon, wear a variety of three-piece lounge suits (266), with stand-up collars and four-in-hand ties. Prunier is a poet. His lounge suit has a velvet jacket, and he wears a bow tie with his wing-collar, to

TOP: Illus. 261; BOTTOM: Illus. 262.

TOP: Illus. 263; BOTTOM, LEFT: Illus. 264; BOTTOM, RIGHT: Illus. 265.

stress his poetic soul (267). Ruggero enters dressed in a three-piece business suit (268) of a color lighter than the others, his figure permitting. If not, a darker vest may break up the solid front. A wing-collar and an attractive four-in-hand tie complete his outfit. After it has been decided that Ruggero is going to spend his first evening in Paris at the Bal Bullier, Magda and Lisette resolve, unbeknownst to each other, that they want to go there as well. When Lisette goes out on the town, she is in the habit of borrowing some suitable attire from her mistress for the occasion (269). The hat and cape she has selected this time are rejected by Prunier out of hand. It is therefore necessary that these items are grotesque and good for a laugh from the audience. The second hat she produces meets with Prunier's approval, but not the cape. Eventually the 'black satin one, she wore the other night' is decided upon. Only, from a practical point of view a mantle is far more suitable than a cape, and that is what Lisette will wear in this production. The lady also has a pocketbook from which she produces various items that will enhance her make-up. As they leave, Prunier has added a cape coat and porkpie felt hat to his suit, rather than the overcoat and tophat the libretto suggests.

Magda intends to go to Bullier in disguise, and a 'Grisette'-type costume seems the logical choice (270). She knows of course that Lisette sometimes helps herself to items of her wardrobe, and decides therefore to turn the tables and 'borrow' a blouse and skirt from her maid. A drastic change of hairdo, a small hat and a shawl and . . . ''Who would ever recognize me?''

ACT II

Bal Bullier is the sort of establishment where diversion seekers from many walks of life gather. Students, artists, grisettes, flowergirls, waiters, mondaines, customers, curiosity seekers (271), and dressmakers are the categories mentioned in the score (272). The grisettes Georgette, Gabrielle, and Lolette are mentioned by name, aside from the principals from the first act: Magda, Lisette, Rambaldo, Prunier, and Ruggero. The latter are all costumed as described previously, except that Rambaldo has added a black topcoat and silk tophat, while Ruggero has donned an additional tweed topcoat and felt Stetson hat.

Either as a result of insufficient heating, or simply because it was the fashion, outdoor clothing—and especially headgear (273)—was

TOP, LEFT: Illus. 266; TOP, RIGHT: Illus. 267; BOTTOM, LEFT: Illus. 268; BOTTOM, RIGHT: Illus. 269.

Illus. 270.

TOP, LEFT: Illus. 271; BOTTOM, RIGHT: Illus. 272.

the common attire in public places, even in the theatre. So it shall be at the Bal Bullier where only the waiters and the flowergirls should go bare-headed. In a crowd scene like this it is the costumer's task to make each group as distinct from the others as possible. At the same time it is very important to make the principals stand out costume-wise, lest they get 'lost in the crowd.' From a color point of view the Bullier scene conjures up visions of Toulouse Lautrec to this listener. The principals will stand out if they do not participate in such a color scheme. Among the grisettes present, Magda might be the only one to carry a shawl. . . . and so on down the line. From their German confreres the students might borrow identical jackets with a faint military air, pants that are identical in color and some kind of pill-box hat gear. Artists are always easily recognized if they wear painter's smocks and berets. Nothing in the dresses of the flowergirls must compete with the colors of the flowers they sell, although an inconspicuous flower wreath in the hair would not be out of place. Waiters most likely wear tail suits and carry a folded white towel over one arm. An elegant 'after theatre' crowd will no doubt be present, with large hats for the ladies, while dressmakers can only be recognized by their inconspicuous clothes and the more showy garments they carry over their arms for delivery, or to sew on, because they did not get them ready on time. And so, a good time is being had by all.

ACT III

No mention has been made in the libretto of the time of the year in which the two previous acts occurred, but Act III takes place "on a magnificent spring day." The locale is a villa on the Riviera. It is late afternoon and tea has been served. Accordingly, Magda wears an elegant afternoon gown of the season (274). If it is possible to express such a sentiment via a costume, the feeling should be conveyed that all is not right. Maybe the color could be surprisingly subdued for the occasion. In truth, despite her genuine affection for Ruggero, Magda is out of her element. Her psychological make-up is that of a demimondaine and she does not adjust well to the role of a faithful lover, try as she may. Ruggero, on the other hand, is very much at home in the surroundings and delighted with the circumstances despite some financial problems. One of the many similarities between the plot of *La*

Illus. 273.

Traviata and *La Rondine* consists in the fact that the male protagonists never earn an honest day's living. They have to rely on financial support from their parents to maintain themselves, and especially their paramours, in the style to which these ladies are accustomed. In his present blissful state Ruggero wears a 'seaside' costume, consisting of light-colored flannel pants with a matching vest, and a harmonizing somewhat darker flannel coat, a turn-down collar and four-in-hand tie.

When Prunier and Lisette appear on the scene they have travelled from Nice and are accordingly in travelling clothes. Especially for Lisette, a duster seems in order (275). Underneath it she wears the same skirt and blouse as in Act I, or something very similar. In that way she can re-emerge from the villa later, complete with cap and apron. These were packed in the suitcase she carried with her inside the villa. And thus, lo and behold, here is Lisette ready to resume her role as Magda's maid: Instead of a duster, Prunier might prefer to wear a tweed knicker-suit with matching hat (276).

The butler, who announced the couple's arrival, wears a butler's daytime suit. It consists of a dark green cutaway coat with metal buttons, matching pants with a narrow yellow stripe on the outside seam, and a yellow-and-green striped vest, also with metal buttons. A wing-collar and green bow tie complete his ensemble.

When Magda emerges from the villa to greet Lisette and Prunier, it would be a good idea if the lady added a shawl to her dress, presumably because it is now late afternoon and the temperature is going down. Actually it is the only way she can make her subsequent departure back to Paris, not merely dressed in spring clothes, which would be highly unlikely.

Illus. 274.

TOP, LEFT: Illus. 275; BOTTOM, RIGHT: Illus. 276.

CHAPTER *12*

STRAUSS'S

Der Rosenkavalier

Illus. 277

*O*NE OF *DER ROSENKAVALIER'S* MEMORABLE features are its numerous waltzes. In 1745, which is the opera's approximate time of action, waltzes did not exist. Strauss was well aware of this. Music-historical fidelity was not uppermost in his mind, however. As a product of his own time he interpreted the Rococo period of Empress Maria Theresa in the terms of his time. Nevertheless it is significant that despite all the waltz music, there is no dancing in *Der Rosenkavalier,* although at one time a short ballet had been contemplated. To observe people waltzing in an 18th-century setting, dressed in 18th-century costumes was evidently considered too much of an anachronism. We, in turn, are products of our own time and cannot fail to interpret the 18th-century's visual aspects, including its costumes from our point of view, which is entirely as it should be.

Alfred Roller's set and costume designs for the opera's world premiere in Dresden in 1911 have been preserved (chapter-opening

244

illustration, 277). What is more, they were published in a production book called 'Regie Skizzen.' Subsequent producers of the opera were compelled to avail themselves of these. Luckily today's producers and designers are free to interpret the opera's visual aspects on their own terms. This does not necessarily mean advancing the time of action as was done—by more than 100 years—by designer Erte for the 1980 Glyndebourne production (278).

It is reported that the staging and acting devised by the famous Max Reinhardt for the 1911 production was nothing short of revolutionary in its realism. Its impact was so great that opera-acting has never been the same since. Yet in this respect also, time does not stand still. Photographs of the opening scene with the original performers in costume reveal Octavian making passionate love, fully clad in coat and boots, to an equally fully robed Marschallin decked out in furs. In our day they still make love in that scene, but they are no longer costumed in that fashion.

In a sense *Der Rosenkavalier* is a study of the mores and manners of three types of nobility. First of all, there are the Marschallin and Octavian, both descendants of long-established noble houses and hence to the manner born. Baron Ochs is a nobleman, but he is a rustic and not very particular about the manners to which he is born. Herr von Faninal is a newcomer to the ranks of nobility. His title was bestowed upon him as a reward, if not in payment, for his services to the crown. While their personal appearances and costumes naturally reflect their status, it will be even more evident from the varying ways their servants are attired.

ACT I

Strauss had the good taste to portray the sexual intercourse between Octavian and the Marschallin solely in musical terms in the opera's introduction. What one witnesses as the curtain rises can fairly be characterized as 'after-play.'

The part of Octavian (279) is written for a female voice, which brings with it certain costume complications. There is a limit to how successfully certain physical female attributes can be disguised, especially if the lady in question is to be clad merely in shirt and breeches, as circumstances demand in this instance. However, the bosom can be bound and hence flattened. (Under no circumstances must a brassiere

TOP, LEFT: Illus. 278; BOTTOM, RIGHT: Illus. 279.

be worn.) 'Symmetricals' can produce more manly-looking calves, and very dark breeches will minimize hips and derriere. Adding the fashionable long vest of that time unbuttoned can also be very helpful. The 'queue' wigs of the period are an additional asset. The fact that this role has been performed successfully by a number of prominent singers proves that with a bit of loving care this change of gender can be accomplished. Actually the male fashions of the mid 18th century, with its long, full-skirted coat and vest are a great asset in that respect. When Octavian returns at the end of this act now fully clothed (280), he wears a kind of riding suit consisting of a velvet coat with three-quarter length, widely cuffed sleeves, which reveal the wrist-ruffled shirt sleeves underneath. The coat may have some frog-like trimming of braid, which gives the outfit a semimilitary air. The breeches match the coat and black boots reach over the knee. The vest, slightly shorter than the coat, may be of a somewhat lighter shade than coat and breeches and of a different fabric, like antique satin. It too has frog-decorations. Octavian now carries the sword which he so carelessly left lying around earlier in the act. The lace edging on his jabot and shirt cuffs should be kept very narrow for the sake of masculinity. In this act his wig is usually a medium brown. He also carries a tricorn under his arm to match his suit. Because headgear worn on top of wigs might ruin the latter's shape, it was usually carried under the arm and hence acquired the name: Chapeau Bras.

Very early in this act Mahomet, the Marschallin's little black-amoor servant (281), arrived on the scene to serve breakfast. He is heralded by the ringing of the silver bells which are attached to his costume, the sound of which the careful listener will detect in the orchestra. He is clad in yellow, quoth the libretto. All that yellow had better be restricted to his turban, his Turkish pants, his sash, and his shirt sleeves. With that he wears an orange-brown knee- length coat of cotton brocade. It has a neck-band collar and its wide sleeves have turned-up cuffs, faced in yellow.

Octavian's 'Mariandl' disguise consists of a laced bodice with tabs, the décolleté filled in by a lace-edged fichu (282). Over the ballerina-length full petticoat, which has some slight hip padding, goes a skirt to match the bodice and an apron to match the fichu. A mob cap which hides the wig's male features also matches fichu and apron. Hose are white and modestly buckled black pumps have a slight heel. One might think that, since Octavian is in reality a woman, now that she is also dressed like a woman, the singer is home free to be quite

TOP, LEFT: Illus. 280; TOP, RIGHT: Illus. 281; BOTTOM: Illus. 282.

herself. It is not quite so simple, for now this woman, who interprets the role of a boy, must act the part of a boy who pretends to be a girl. While the performer's acting ability must create that illusion by and large, a few costume tricks may help: the shoulders should be made to look somewhat too square for a girl, and the waist a little too thick. The hip-padding should be kept to a minimun also. It is only because Baron Ochs is not very discriminating in such details that he is oblivious to these masculine characteristics.

The notion that Octavian finds his Mariandl disguise in a closet in the Marschallin's room is absurd. No self-respecting Marschallin keeps servant's attire in her closet. The libretto mentions the existence of some almost invisible doors in her room. Tourists visiting European castles and palaces may have observed such doors. They invariably conceal a labyrinth of corridors and stairways leading to the servants' quarters. They also served as an entrance-and exit-way for clandestine visitors. There can be no doubt that Octavian obtained his Mariandl disguise by travelling that route. It is the only thing that makes sense.

There are in the English language no words for the German titles 'Fuerst' and 'Fuerstin' except Prince and Princess, to which 'of the Realm' should be added to distinguish them from Royalty. That the Princess of Werdenberg is a 'Feldmarschallin' (283) does not imply that she is a female Feldmarschall, but rather that she is married to one. According to the libretto this lady is dressed in a 'lace night-gown' at the curtain's rising. A lace nightgown is an unlikely garment for anyone in the 18th century, when the average night attire was still mostly utilitarian. Marie Therese's may have been of silk with some lace trim on it, but that would be about the extent of it. Upon arising she adds a complementary ample negligee (284), which may have the customary flattering lace engageantes, bows, and even some fur trim. Ladies were never 'en negligee' without a suitable haircovering, and the Marschallin also must wear an elegant 'Baigneuse' until it is removed later on by her Hairdresser.

Shortly before the entrance of the 'levee's' participants, the 'antichambre' as they are referred to in the text, an old woman, evidently the Marschallin's dresser, enters, in order to change the latter's costume for one more suitable for the events to come. According to the customs it must still be a negligee, but much more elaborate than the previous one (285). It consists of a bow-trimmed stomacher and a slightly paniered underskirt under an elaborate sheer 'flying gown' with a Watteau back. It would be a nice touch if the old lady

TOP: Illus. 283; BOTTOM: Illus. 284.

carried it over her arm upon entering. She in turn is dressed in a much darker and older version of Mariandl's costume, with a voluminous mob cap, and equally voluminous fichu and apron. These accessories might even be in black sheer.

It has been pointed out that Baron Ochs is not 'von' Lerchenau, but 'auf' Lerchenau. This subtle difference indicates that he is not the owner of the Lerchenau estate and castle but rather its permanent tenant, which puts him on a fairly low rung of the nobility ladder. From today's moral point of view he is no doubt a lecher, but within the realm of 18th-century morality, he is merely a man with a one-track mind. Otherwise his cousin the Marschallin would have reacted with indignation to the endless tirades of his amorous conquests. Instead, she is merely mildly amused. Ochs' rustic character should find expression in his clothes, which are of the tweedy, leathery kind, at least in this act (286). For his cousin the Marschallin he does not feel compelled to put on a show, and his clothes should have an improvised air. The tweed coat may have some leather trim down the front and on the cuffs. The breeches do not match, but neither do they clash. The same applies to his vest, which might be of suede. His jabot and sleeve ruffles sport but a minimum of lace. His boots are knee high, his felt tricorn adheres to the general color scheme. A sword is optional in this act, although noblemen were rarely without one.

The Marschallin's servants are not in 'grande tenue' in this act, but wear dignified identical lackey uniforms of the period (287), that fit within the color scheme of the set. If the suits were not identical they would be indistinguishable from other male attire of the period. They all wear identical simple white bag wigs, white hose, black buckled shoes, lace jabots, and cuff ruffles. Struhan, the Marschallin's Major Domo, wears a lackey uniform identical to the other servants in cut and color, but his is elaborately gold braided. He wears an order-sash and aiguillettes on one shoulder. His shoes have gold buckles, and his is a queue wig. His lace jabot and sleeve ruffles are somewhat more profuse. He is exceedingly dignified.

The 'levee' participants (288) consist of a Notary, the Head-cook and a Kitchen-aid, the Milliner, a Scholar, the Animal Seller, the intriguers Valzacchi and Annina, a Noble Widow with her three children, the Singer, and the Flute Player. A little later the Hairdresser and his Assistant also appear as well as Baron Och's retinue. This odd assemblage is a costumer's opportunity for varied and colorful costume characterization without going into caricature. In casting these

TOP: Illus. 285; BOTTOM, LEFT: Illus. 286; BOTTOM, RIGHT: Illus. 287.

characters the goal should be to achieve as much physical contrast as possible for the costumer to exploit.

The Notary wears a plain black coat vest and breeches, hose, and shoes. Instead of a jabot he wears judicial tabs, which implies that his vest is buttoned all the way to the neck. He wears a short full-bottomed wig, and has a goose quill behind one ear. Under his arm is a wide-brimmed black hat.

The Head-cook is all in white, with the customary cook's apron and hat, although the latter may have a more beret-like crown to give it that 'period feeling.'

The Kitchen-aid is in his shirt sleeves, under a cotton vest and dark cotton breeches, which are partly covered with a tied around half-apron. His hose are grey. His hair is tied in back with a string.

The Milliner wears a chic but simple Polonaise (289). She knows her place and does not want to compete with her customers. Yet her headdress is fairly elaborate, as behooves a milliner. On ribbons over either arm she carries large hat boxes, and in each hand she displays a spectacular hat.

Everything about the Scholar is grey: his very long cloth coat, vest and breeches, his hose, his short fullbottomed wig, and even his complexion has a greyish hue about it. He also wears spectacles. His jabot and wrist ruffles arc cotton.

The Animal Seller is a tradesman in rough, loose fitting, dark woolen clothes, of which the individual parts neither match nor clash. He wears cloth leggings, rough shoes, and a rough straw hat under his arm. The only thing spectacular about him are the various animals he carries. The more variety the merrier.

Professional intriguers are a product of 18th-century morality, when "Liaisons Dangereuses" were the order of the day and sleazy characters could make a living by being conspiring informants, who display short-lived loyalty only to the highest bidder. The use of 'changeant' fabrics seems appropos for these shifty characters; dark solid ones for Valzacchi, and dark-flowered ones for Annina (290). He will whisper his secrets behind the tricorn he carries in his hand, while Annina will avail herself of a black-lace stole, which she carries draped over her head, and of a fan, for the same purpose. She also wears black-lace mittens, and the hair color of both these Italians is: black.

The "three poor, noble orphans" (291) are not orphans at all, for they are accompanied by a very much alive widowed mother. Since

TOP: Illus. 288; BOTTOM: Illus. 289.

they make a spectacle of their poverty, and are therefore rewarded with a filled purse by the Marschallin, their mourning attire must be of the very simplest, Mama's included (292). That does not mean that it is not modestly fashionable in silhouette, and that all the accessories are not accounted for, including black headdresses, hose, and shoes, as well as little ribbons around the neck. The only items not black are their handkerchiefs, of which they avail themselves profusely to wipe their tears.

"The first act is not over until the fat tenor sings" to paraphrase a popular saying. Yet, unless the singer cast for the part has naturally the necessary avoirdupois to fit that description, he may not want to be padded to execute this difficult aria. An alternate solution is to make him look as florid as his music sounds (293). As a true professional this gentleman feels that his singing here is 'a performance' for which occasion he wears the appropriate theatrical costume. The coat is of an unsubtle flowered brocade, the cuffs, pocket flaps, vest, and breeches are of velvet, on which gold braid and gold buttons have not been spared. Hose are white, the shoes have gold buckles, and the white queue wig has lavish curls in back.

The Flute Player by contrast is a poor schlemiel whose status is not above that of a servant and who ekes out an existence playing flute obligati for famous singers. He wears a nondescript three-piece cloth suit. If everything on the Scholar was grey, everything on the Flute Player is beige, including his hair, his hose, and his complexion.

The Hairdresser, Hippolyte (294), is not really part of the 'levee,' but actually comes to dress the Marschallin's hair. He is an elegant somewhat effeminate man, who reluctantly doffed his coat while at work, but still reveals under his apron a brocade vest, harmonizing breeches and a lavish lace-trimmed shirt and jabot. To say that his wig is in the latest style is putting it mildly. As has been remarked earlier, the Hairdresser's main function is to remove the Marschallin's Baigneuse. Underneath, her hair is already dressed for the day, and Hippolyte only has to go through the motions of dressing it. After the Marschallin complains that he made her look like an old woman, he usually hysterically fools around a little more, without realy changing anything. It would be much more effective if he could indeed accomplish a change, which is noticeable to the audience. If, for instance, a few curls which were at first pinned up could now be let down to form the well-known 'side curls,' this would have indeed a softening effect and make a more youthful impression.

TOP: Illus. 290; BOTTOM: Illus. 291.

TOP: Illus. 292; BOTTOM: Illus. 293.

Illus. 294.

No sooner has the Hairdresser started his labors than "a courier enters in a livery of pink, silver and black, carrying a note." The significance of this incident is never made clear. The note is eventually used to cool a curling iron. One may assume that the courier's coat was pink, his vest silver, and his breeches black.

Hippolyte's assistant is a small hyperactive young lad, dressed in shirt, vest, and breeches. He too wears an apron, and his own hair is carefully styled.

Baron Ochs' 'retinue' can hardly be called such. It consists of only three people: his body-servant Leopold, actually his illegitimate son (295); an almoner (296); and a huntsman (297). For the occasion they have donned ill-fitting livery coats, to which their own rough and tumble clothes have no connection. Their unkempt hair is tied in the back with a string.

ACT II

The temptation exists to think of 'von' Faninal as a 'nouveau riche,' which is a mistake. He is instead a 'nouveau noble,' (298) to coin a phrase. He may have been 'riche' for quite a while already. He is eager to follow all the rules his newly acquired title imposes, although he still has to be admonished that a mere 'Herr von . . .' walks three paces behind the superior nobility of a 'Baron auf . . . .' Faninal comes across as a man of conservative taste, who dresses accordingly. Yet, the occasion of receiving his future son-in-law demand at least a 'Sunday-best' attire, which is expressed in a subdued brocade coat, with a complementary vest and solid velvet breeches. His sleeve cuffs and pocket flaps are of the same velvet and are moderately braid-decorated. His jabot is profuse, as are his shirt sleeves and cuff ruffles. He carries a sword and wears a long, brown full-bottomed wig. His black shoes have square high heels.

Sophie's character displays a combination of humility, strength, and moral fiber. She, too, is dressed for the occasion in an elegant, but youthful and simple 'Robe à l'Anglaise' over a paniered underskirt and stomacher (299). Pale yellow seems a suitable color for her. The gown is modestly trimmed with matching ruffles and bows. The sleeves naturally show the white lace 'engageantes' and, the length of the neck of the performer permitting, a small lace double ruffle and

TOP, LEFT: Illus. 295; BOTTOM, RIGHT: Illus. 296.

Illus. 297.

Illus. 298.

yellow velvet ribbon are called for as well as a vestigial matching headdress. Moderately high heeled shoes must also match.

Marianne Leitmetzerin, Sophie's duenna, is presumably a middle-aged spinster lady, though her age and marital status are nowhere mentioned. Her reportage of Faninal's departure and Octavian's subsequent arrival involve her in one of Strauss's favorite pastimes: anticipation music. By the time Octavian makes his entrance he really has something to live up to, after the way his pending arrival was heralded. Marianne is a very proper lady who is accordingly very properly gowned in a paniered, deep mauve taffeta 'Robe à l'Anglaise,' with black lace trimming, 'engageantes,' fichu and headdress (300). One of her remarks concerns the color of the curtains of von Faninal's equipage. They are sky-blue, which strikes one as an excellent color for his lackeys' uniforms, for it is through the attire of his servants that this newcome nobleman hopes to impress his newly acquired equals.

His Major Domo (301), who proved so well versed in noble etiquette, wears accordingly a sky-blue velvet coat, braided in black and silver, a silver vest, equally braided and black satin breeches. Black, silver-buckled shoes, a lace jabot and lace-trimmed shirt sleeves would complete his costume were it not for silver aiguilettes, a shoulder sash, a short full-bottomed wig, and white gloves. The lackeys under his command wear a modified version of his costume (301). Their coats and vests are of blue and grey cloth respectively, modestly braided in black and silver. Breeches are of black cloth and their lingerie is more modest also. They wear white tye-bag wigs and white gloves.

Upon his much heralded entrance Marianne describes Octavian as: "All in silver, glittering from head to toe." (302) In costumer's parlance that means: A coat of silver brocade, ornamented with silver sequins and rhinestones. His vest and breeches are of silver moire, the former equally ornamented. The jabot and cuff ruffles are of silver lace. His silver shoes have rhinestone buckles, he carries a sword, and last but not least, he has changed his brown queue wig for a white one, not an uncommon occurrence in those days.

His retinue, dressed in the Rofrano colors of white and pale green, consists of lackeys, couriers, and Heyducks. The lackeys wear white coats and vests, trimmed with pale green braid, and matching pale green breeches. Furthermore, they wear white hose, black shoes, and white queue wigs with black bows. The couriers are clad in

TOP, LEFT: Illus. 299; TOP, RIGHT: Illus. 300; BOTTOM: Illus. 301.

hip-length white coats and vests, trimmed with pale green braid and shoulder fringe, which is repeated at the bottom of the white breeches. Over this a pale green chamois 'rhinegrave'-type skirt is worn. Helmets consist of metal frontals behind which pale green ostrich plumes rise up. They also carry tall canes.

'Heyducks' (303) were originally Hungarian soldiers, whose uniforms remained popular in some retinues. Over white uniforms, with pale greenbraid trimming at the thighs, goes a white jacket, heavily braided with greencord in military fashion. The white fur-edged sling-cape-coat, lined in pale green is similarly braided. A white fur shako has a hanging fall, ending in a green tassel. A green ostrich plume tops the shako. A curved saber and calf-high white boots complete this costume. The Negro servant who carries Octavian's tricorn, wears a modified Heyduck's uniform.

Baron Ochs is all dressed up for the occasion in a richly gold embroidered satin coat and vest, with breeches in a darker complementary color (304). He too has changed his brown wig for a white one, and he too carries a sword.

Ochs' retinue wear the same rough woolen lackey coats they sported in Act I, but have now added complementary vests and breeches, which are equally ill fitting. Their number has increased to six. One of them has a big plaster bandage on his nose according to the libretto. They are in hot pursuit of Faninal's female servants, who might be wearing pale blue laced bodices, fully petticoated blue and white striped skirts over hip pads. Also white, lace-edged aprons, fichus and mob caps. To be able to differentiate between cooks, scrubwomen and chambermaids, variations of the costume first described can be used, like solid blue skirts, with striped bodices and aprons, and/or striped skirts with blue aprons, etc., so long as they form a unit colorwise.

The Notary repeats his Act I costume, while the doctor is clad in a three-piece black cloth suit, with a short white, full-bottomed wig.

Annina and Valzacchi repeat their Act I costumes.

ACT III

Annina is the first person the audience perceives as the curtain rises for Act III to reveal the private room in an inn. She is in the process of arranging the widow's weeds (305, right) she has donned as

caleçon de lin, une tuni-
que collante appelée
koutonet, entourée d'une ceinture, l'abnet. Grand prêtre hébreu.

Heiduque, livrée du prince
de Condé (1776).

Haïdouk, garde du Corps
(Hongrie, 1748).

TOP, LEFT: Illus. 302; TOP, RIGHT: Illus. 303; BOTTOM: Illus. 304.

part of the upcoming charade. It is a modest black 'Robe à l'Anglaise,' somewhat more elaborate than the one worn by the poor widow of the Act I levee. It includes her black-lace mittens, a black headdress, and mourning veil. Valzacchi, who assists her in arranging the dress, requires no change of costume, although a black cape might abet his conspiratorial air.

Octavian is preceded upon his entrance by an elderly lady, very reminiscent of the dresser in Act I, who helped the Marschallin change negligees. Her function here is not made clear. Octavian is again in 'Mariandl' disguise (305, left), but for this auspicious occasion it is a little more formal than the Act I improvisation, although the masculine square shoulders and somewhat thick waist are still apparent. He too has returned to his original hair color and hair styling, which may or may not be a wig. Its masculine features are again concealed by the chambermaid headdress. An important feature of this Mariandl dress is the long skirt which conceals the boots he wears over ankle tights. From the pocket of the latter, Octavian produces a purse which he proceeds to give to Valzacchi. The customary sheer, lace-edged fichu and apron are again part of the Mariandl costume.

The importance of these accessories lies in the fact that they are later on thrown, one by one, over the top of the bedstead's curtain, together with the dress, petticoat, and hip pads, for the charade's ultimate denouement.

Five 'suspicious looking men' next appear on the scene. It has to be determined what it is about these men's looks and behavior that arouses suspicion. Either or both must convey the message that they do not belong in these surroundings (306a,b,c). They may be a bunch of misshapen beggars which Valzacchi picked up in the street somewhere and for a handout will do his bidding. Then again they may be some of Octavian's servants who have been pressed into service for the occasion. In the case of the former they may be clad in their own rags, while the latter may don domino-like garments supplied by Valzacchi. In either circumstance the colors must be dark and ominous, a somewhat mottled mixture of black, khaki and dark grey, while the scary face masks Valzacchi supplies will do the rest.

Next on the 'entrance' list are the inn's waiters. They wear identical cloth coats buttoned to the neck, with harmonizing cloth breeches. Half aprons are tied around the waist. Their lingerie is made of cotton, their own hair is tied in back and they carry a folded towel

Illus. 305.

over the arm. The kitchen boy is colorwise identical to the waiters, but he wears a vest instead of a coat and is in his shirt sleeves.

Baron Ochs carries his wounded arm in a sling. Otherwise his costume is of the rustic type, like the one he wore in Act I. It may even be a repeat. The brown wig he removes later on in the act is also repeated from Act I. That upon removal of the wig he reveals a bald pate, does not indicate that his own hair fell out, but rather that he is shaven bald as was the custom for all wig-wearing men. Contemporary French paintings always give the impression that the fashionable wigs of that period fit the wearers as if it were their own hair. Illustrations from other countries tend to be more realistic in that respect and frequently reveal a five o'clock shadow on top of the head, where the wearer's natural hairline and that of the wig did not coincide.

Leopold, Baron Ochs' illegitimate son, repeats his Act II lackey costume.

The Innkeeper wears a simple but dignified three-piece cloth suit, with a modest jabot and sleeve ruffles. On his head is a short, grey, full-bottomed wig.

The offspring of Ochs' and Annina's alleged union are four children: age two, four, six, and eight years. They are two boys and two girls (307), it is assumed. In the 18th century children were clothed like miniature grown-ups and so it must be in this case. Childhood pictures of young Mozart and his sister can serve as examples, although clothes a little less fancy than theirs will suffice.

The Police, such as it was, and the Military were clothed very similarly in that period. The Police Commissioner might wear a navy blue coat with red front panels, red vewt, pocket flaps and cuffs. It would all be trimmed with white braid and gold buttons. His ankle tights are white, his knee-high boots black. He carries a sword on a wide leather bandoleer. His black tricorn, edged in white, has a red cockade on the left side. His tye-bag wig is of a natural color. The Policemen's coats match the Commissioner's but omit the red. Their vests are also blue, their ankle tights white. Instead of boots they wear black cloth leggings. Their leather sword belts are narrow, their black tricorns plain, while their tye-bag wigs are also of a natural hair color.

Von Faninal has added a voluminous cape to match his Act II costume (308).

The Guests at the inn, who come to see what the deuce is going on, wear a variety of upper-middle class clothes of the period (309a,b). Many of the ladies top their frilly caps with straw hats. The men wear

Illus. 306a.

TOP: 306b; BOTTOM: 306c.

Illus. 307.

a variety of queue wigs and full-bottomed wigs in different hair colors, and carry their tricorns under the arm.

The Musicians emulate in dress the Flute player from the levee, but vary the colors.

Sophie wears a young woman's simple but elegant Robe à l'Anglaise (310), not unlike the one from Act II. For outdoor purposes she has added a lace stole, and her lace handkerchief must not be forgotten, lest the opera never ends.

Von Faninal's footmen repeat their Act II attire.

The Marschallin's entrance must be impressive. Since Mahomet carries her train, it is most likely a stately, fur trimmed Robe à la Française with a Watteau back (311). In her mood of resignation she has chosen a more subdued color. The miniature tricorn hat, so familiar to us from the photographs of Mme. Lotte Lehmann in the role, is also entirely appropriate. It is important, not merely that the colors of the trio harmonize, but that The Marschallin's and Von Faninal's also complement each other.

When Octavian emerges at last in male attire, he has added to his Act I costume a matching velvet cape, which not only covers his own back, but which he spreads over Sophie's shoulder as they leave the stage.

Mahomet ends the opera in his one and only costume, silver bells and all.

Illus. 308.

TOP: Illus. 309a; BOTTOM: Illus. 309b.

TOP, LEFT: Illus. 310; BOTTOM, RIGHT: Illus. 311.

CHAPTER *13*

STRAUSS'S

Salome

Illus. 312

*I*T HAS LONG BEEN this writer's contention that musical sound, to those who are sensitive to it, will conjure up visual imagery. There is no more striking example of this than a comparison between reading Oscar Wilde's play *Salome,* which he wrote in 1893 in French, and listening to Strauss's *Salome,* the libretto of which the composer distilled from a German translation of Wilde's play in 1903. The play produces visions of Aubrey Beardsley's illustrations (chapter-opening illustration, 312) in the mind's eye of this reader, although the author himself is supposed to have been inspired by the Salome paintings of Gustave Moreau (313). Strauss's *Salome* music, on the other hand, conjures up visions of Gustav Klimt's paintings (314) in this listener's mind. Naturally such visions will vary from person to person, which makes it all the more exciting. Strauss rarely expressed himself concerning the visual aspects of his operas until he began to collaborate with Hugo von Hofmannsthal, who appeared on the scene right

TOP, LEFT: Illus. 313; BOTTOM, RIGHT: Illus. 314.

after *Salome* and was to remain his librettist for six operas. In his 'Recollections' Strauss wrote the following anent *Salome* (translation by the author): "For a long time already I have found fault with the Oriental-Jewish operas in that they are lacking in authentic oriental coloring and glowing sun. That need inspired truly exotic harmonies in me, which I painted especially in strange cadences like 'changeant silk'." For the 1928 production of *Die Aegyptisch Helena,* an opera which is also based on a story from Antiquity, Von Hoffmannsthal expressed himself as follows on the subject: "As for the costumes, especially those of Helen and Aithra, they subtly must consist in their not simply being dull antique trappings but approaching modern evening dress. I take it from 'Vogue' that this winter a lot of glittering gold and silver materials will be worn again. This kind of thing will have to make up Aithra's wardrobe. Perhaps Fanto has a real flair for such a thing." The 'Fanto' Von Hofmannsthal is referring to was Leonhard Fanto, a scenic artist attached to the Royal Dresden Opera House. *Salome* was the first of six operas he designed for Strauss. The last one was *Daphne* in 1938. There is no doubt that Strauss and Von Hofmannsthal would have advocated the same approach toward the *Salome* costumes.

Salome can serve as a role model for the path opera costume designers must travel. Historically the opera's main characters, Salome, Jokanaan, Herod, and Herodias all existed. With considerable trouble it is possible to ascertain what people wore around 30 A.D. (315) in the town of Macherus, in Judea, where Herod Antipas ruled at that time. 'With considerable trouble' because for reasons unknown there is a documentation gap between about 500 B.C. and 500 A.D. Luckily clothes changed so gradually at that time, that a few hundred years in either direction seems to have little impact. The first thing to be established is what the character in question would authentically have worn at that time, modified by the role's personal characteristics, and the way that role fits into the overall picture. All this must then be modified by the visual imagery conjured up by the music. Ultimately a performer's personality and physical attributes will also have an impact. In his book *Richard Strauss, the Staging of His Operas and Ballets* (New York: Oxford Univ. Pr.) the noted stage-director Rudolf Hartmann observed the following apropos of the painting of a scene from *Salome's* world premiere: ". . . The figures at the palace entrance almost overpower the principal performers and there is little evidence of any attempts to contrast the groups of Romans, Egyptians, Jews,

Illus. 315.

etc.'' It is exactly such pitfalls which the successful costume designer will manage to avoid.

Narraboth is the Syrian Captain of the Guard who cannot keep his eyes off Salome. His good looks are mentioned in the play. He had better be a good actor as well, for his Roman Captain's uniform (316) is not helpful in revealing his vulnerability to the princess' charms. It is not clear in what manner he eventually kills himself, for Roman soldiers were not equipped with daggers, but rather carried swords. The safest way will be for him to carry out the fatal deed while his back is turned toward the audience.

The two bored Roman soldiers, one of whom has some kind words to say about his prisoner, wear Roman soldier's attire naturally (317). It is assumed that there will be more of their kind around when they are ultimately called upon to crush Salome, for which occasion they must be equipped with shields.

The role of the Page is sung by a woman. Hers is the voice of doom, warning constantly of the dire events which are in the offing. A brief, dark toga over a slightly lighter, belted tunic will convey that feeling (318). It will at the same time mask any female attributes. It is logical to assume that there are more pages in Herod's suite who will be dressed identically, but their costumes can be of lighter shades. Roman sandals laced up the leg till below the knee will harmonize with that as well as Roman-style hairdos rather than any headgear. In general everybody wears sandals in this opera, while Salome removes hers just prior to her dance.

Ideally the part of Jokanaan (John the Baptist) should be portrayed by a tall, slender singer, for that is the way he is described in the text. He is dressed merely in a camelhair shirt and leather belt (319). His hair and beard are long and dark. Because in opera vocal suitability takes precedence over physical appropriateness, he may have to be clad in a more loose-fitting voluminous robe, which must bear the marks of his long imprisonment. The condition of the stage floor permitting, he should be barefoot.

According to the *Encyclopedia Americana* a 'Cappadocian' is a light-skinned Syrian (320). In the play more so than in the opera he behaves like a tourist in a foreign country, who constantly asks questions but is not afraid to express his opinions. Giving him a somewhat foreign looking costume might therefore be appropriate, although it should by no means be bizarre, nor attract attention. His is a minor role.

TOP, LEFT: Illus. 316; BOTTOM, RIGHT: Illus. 317.

TOP, LEFT: Illus. 318; BOTTOM, RIGHT: Illus. 319.

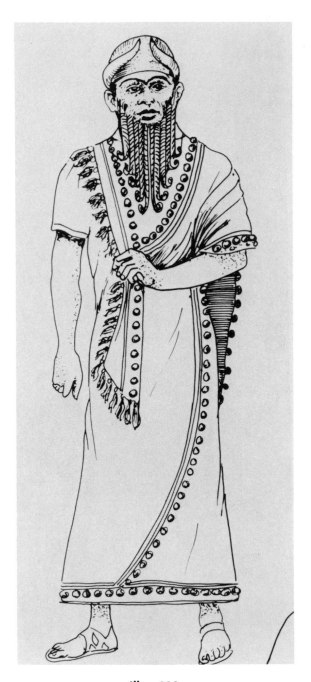

Illus. 320.

The only character in the opera who has a change of costume is Salome herself. Actually it does not even have to be a complete 'change of costume.' When she is ready to start her dance before Herod, slaves merely bring perfume, the seven veils, and remove her sandals. The costume Salome wears upon her first appearance must convey the impression of extreme purity and innocence. It consists of a gown and a cloak. The latter may be of a lightweight fabric but not transparent, unlike the 'muslin veil' she promises Narraboth to smile through if he produces Jokanaan before her. When in her attempt to seduce the Prophet she removes the cloak, it may become apparent that the gown under it is far more revealing than was at first assumed (321). The figure of the performer permitting, the wearing of a basic bodystocking underneath everything else would solve many problems. Too much depends on the stage-director–choreographer's approach to the entire 'dance of the seven veils,' not to mention the performer's prowess in such matters to make any valid suggestions in that respect. Suffice it to say that this observer has found total nudity on the stage a highly overrated pastime. As 'Burlesque' has taught us, it is the removal of items of clothing that is seductive rather than the bare facts.

According to Jokanaan, Herod (322) will die in a mantle of silver, but that event does not occur in the opera. Herod is an Edomite who was raised in Rome. On this particular occasion he is drunk and delirious, but as the Tetrach of Galilea and Perea, he is a person of consequence and at the moment he hosts a banquet for numerous foreigners. Accordingly, he can be expected to be dressed in robes of state, mantle and crown, all of them somewhat in disarray owing to his besotted condition. It is pointed out that he also wears a wreath of red roses, which he tears off in a fit of annoyance.

One of the many questions the Cappadocian asks in the play is whether "she who wears a black mitre sewed with pearls, and whose hair is powdered with blue dust" is Queen Herodias (322). It is indeed, and it may be considered a good start for that lady's attire. A dark, much bejewelled robe under an equally adorned, sheer, draped mantle will do justice to the character and music of this decadent first lady of a very decadent court. Both she and Salome carry fans, according to the libretto. It is a rather anachronistic notion. Some antique version of that accessory will have to be used, for Salome hides her face behind it while Herodias uses it to hit one of her slaves on the head.

TOP, LEFT: Illus. 321; BOTTOM, RIGHT: Illus. 322.

An anklelength wrap-around piece of cloth with some fringe on the bottom and a head band will serve those ladies well.

It is helpful if each group of guests at the banquet has a costume feature through which a modern audience can identify them. For the Jews (323) black Yarmulkas might serve to that end. Because they are constantly at cross purposes, one might take advantage of the popularity of striped fabrics at that time, for their robes. Only some should be striped horizontally, some vertically, and some diagonally. That will really get the message across.

Oscar Wilde observes that the Egyptian guests wear fine linen robes, shining with hyacinth stones (324). In addition they carry shields of gold. Elsewhere in the play 'russet cloaks' are mentioned for the Egyptians. From these hints one might distill: Russet robes with the typical decorative Egyptian collar and apron and added to that the 'Khat' headdress. The jewelled stone decorations had better be reserved for the host and hostess, while the shields remain the Roman soldiers' exclusive accessory.

The Roman guests, on whom Salome heaps such scorn, wear, odd as it may seem, Roman togas draped over their long tunics (325). In order to be able to identify them as a group it helps if the tunics are all identical in color, while the togas have a decorative laurel leaf band at the edge. The curly, combed-forward Roman hairstyles will suit them as well.

Although Christianity had not yet been promulgated as a religion at that time, it is evident that the Nazarenes (326) have adopted that creed. Accordingly, the simple ample robes in the way Christ is usually depicted would be suitable for them.

The Executioner is named Naaman according to Wilde's play and he is described therein as 'a huge negro.' In the opera the race of the Executioner is never referred to, but a stage direction mentions: "A huge black arm of the Executioner, comes forth from the cistern. . . ." In medieval times executioners were frequently hooded figures, dressed entirely in black (327). One might prefer to opt for this approach in an opera whose symbolism transcends its time in history.

TOP, LEFT: Illus. 323; BOTTOM, RIGHT: Illus. 324.

TOP, LEFT: Illus. 325; BOTTOM, RIGHT: Illus. 326.

Illus. 327.

Illus. 328

CHAPTER *14*

PUCCINI'S

Il Trittico: Il Tabarro, Suor Angelica, and Gianni Schicchi

*P*UCCINI'S *IL TRITTICO* IS UNIQUE in the annals of opera history. No other combination of three one-act operas, intended to be performed as one production, seems to exist. The costumer who embarks on investigating sources of relevant information which can be material to their visual realization will unearth very little pertinent data. The only absolutely certain fact is that the events of *Gianni Schicchi* took place in 1299 when Dante referred to that character in the *Inferno* section of *La Divina Commedia*.

Whether the order in which the operas were performed at their world premiere in 1918 at the Metropolitan Opera in New York is mandatory is not known, but a shift in the order might affect the visual balance and hence the costumes. The same is true if the operas are performed individually or in combination with other one-act operas.

291

Suor Angelica especially may require a different color value in such events as will be discussed later.

Some arduous detective work has unveiled exciting clues regarding the two other partners in this 'triptych.' These findings will be evaluated when each opera is discussed individually.

IL TABARRO

Adami based the libretto for *Il Tabarro* on the one-act play by Didier Gold, 'La Houppeland,' which Puccini had seen in Paris in 1912. He started composing the opera in 1913, and one clue concerning the time of its events is the sound of an auto horn in the orchestra. The use of auto horns in Paris traffic was forbidden in later years. 1912 seems, therefore, the logical time for the opera, except for one fly in that ointment: 1912 was the year 'hobble skirts' were in fashion for women. Although the female characters in *Il Tabarro* are hardly fashion models, they would nevertheless have adopted the fashionable silhouette of the day, except La Frugola. A hobble skirt, particularly for Giorgietta, seems to suit neither her character nor her music. Puccini himself is reported to have favored a red polka dot blouse for the opera's tragic heroine. Whereas his intentions were no doubt honorable, something not quite so obvious seems more suitable. A blouse and skirt are entirely appropriate for Giorgietta's workaday attire (chapter-opening illustration, 328), while going back but a year or two before the hobble skirts will solve that problem. It will not affect the men's clothes in any way. Stevedores are not known to be very fashion conscious, not even in Paris.

Workaday attire or not, Giorgietta's skirt and blouse must have a seductive allure. It must be believable that Michele, who is 25 years her senior and Luigi, who is five years younger than she, both succumbed to her charms. This costumer once successfully combined for Giorgietta a dark red blouse with a dark mauve skirt, united by a dark green belt. For the last scene a complementary shawl should be added. While she is hanging up the laundry in the opening scene Giorgietta would logically wear an apron, which she will have removed when she returns with the wine.

Michele, the barge's captain, has appropriately a rough 'merchant marine' look about him, all in navy blue (329). With a marine visor cap he may wear corduroy pants and jacket, possibly a vest or a sweater, over a collarless neckband shirt, which can reveal long underwear at the neck and wrists. His 'tabarro' (330) is of the darkest navy blue wool, very long and very ample. It may have a turn-over stand-up collar.

There is no such thing as a 'Stevedore' costume. Men like Luigi, Tinca (331), Talpa (332), and the gentlemen of the ensemble wear on this occasion whatever workmen in Paris wore at that time: cloth pants and short jackets, preferably not matching, sometimes vests, sometimes sweaters, collarless neckband shirts, and sometimes in lieu of these only long underwear. Smocks which had been so popular in the past for children and grown-ups, were still in use. It seems just the right thing for Tinca, and for a few chorus members. An occasional work apron will also be useful, nor will a few knitted scarves hurt anyone. It seems especially right for Talpa, who is otherwise in dark, rough-looking clothes with much long underwear showing. Cloth visorcaps were worn without exception. Shoes were ankle high, laced, black, round-toed and worn-looking.

To make Luigi (333) stand out favorably from the crowd, he might be the only one in vest and pants, sans jacket until the final scene when he carries the jacket over his shoulder. His physical attributes permitting his shirt sleeves could be rolled up to reveal bare arms, while his unbuttoned neckband shirt could also show a bit of skin. No long underwear for Luigi! The colors of his clothes are lighter than the others. The individual parts harmonize but do not match.

A ragged smock or ditto frockcoat, a scarf, and a beaten up bowler hat will suit the actor who plays the old Organ Grinder (334). He/she also has to learn not to turn the handle of his/her hurdy-gurdy in time with the music, because it is a machine, not a musical instrument. This writer learned that the hard way when he perpetrated the part of the Organ Grinder in his student days.

Frugola's name implies not merely that she is a jolly person (335) but also that she is a rummager, while the libretto states that she is in rags but presents a characteristic figure. Translated into costume terms that means that she wears a ragged, once-fashionable dress discarded by its wealthy owner and picked up by the rummaging Frugola. It should be of a dark color but not necessarily black. Giorgietta has mentioned the chilly evening air, wherefore a shawl is in order for Frugola.

TOP, LEFT: Illus. 329; BOTTOM, RIGHT: Illus. 330.

TOP: Illus. 331; BOTTOM, LEFT: Illus. 332; BOTTOM, RIGHT: Illus. 333.

Illus. 334.

Illus. 335.

298 • *Costuming for Opera*

The Song Peddler makes a modest attempt at being a dandy to impress his audience. This can be accomplished by letting him be the only one who wears a Hoover collar and bow tie with his neckband shirt. He also wears a low-crowned derby or a porkpie hat. The Midinettes are fashionably, though modestly, dressed, some in dresses, some in blouses and skirts, some in suits. They all wear hats. It is assumed that the song peddler and one of the Midinettes will double as the shadowy lovers who pass briefly later in the scene.

SUOR ANGELICA

The libretto of *Suor Angelica* is an original story; thus the late 17th century as the time of its occurrence is the librettist's invention. It is an unfortunate choice for two reasons: it would require the nuns to wear voluminous petticoats to conform with the female silhouette of that time. To convince oneself that even nuns' costumes conform to prevailing fashions in a modest way, one only has to observe the lengths of nuns' skirts in our day. The soft and fluid lines of late 17th-century women's dress would rob Angelica's aunt, the Princess, of the look of austere rigidity her character demands. The straightlaced silhouette of the early 20th century would suit her much better and would not interfere visually with the nuns' costumes in any way.

Those in charge of the visual aspects of a production of *Il Trittico* will want to strike a balance between the three operas. Only in the case of *Suor Angelica* is it possible to attain a difference in appearance, depending on the order in which the operas are performed or whether it is combined with another one-act opera by another composer. If such is the case, this difference can be accomplished by changing the basic color of the nuns' habits in order to achieve a balance with the general tone of the other operas which it is combined with or surrounded by. Acceptable colors for nuns' habits are: black, white, brown, grey, and blue.

Although we tend to think of the clothes of the Catholic clergy as black, especially those worn for nonofficiating purposes, this was by no means always so. As was mentioned above, in the case of nuns' attire aside from black (always with white accessories), blue, grey, brown, and white, and combinations thereof were frequently used for their habits, and in a few instances they still are. The opera's libretto twice makes mention of the nuns' 'white habits.' The use of white for all the nuns throughout the opera must be considered unwise from a theatrical-visual point of view. A mass of white costumes on the stage for any length of time easily has a blinding effect, is difficult to light, and becomes boring. The use of an occasional white costume can be very effective. The costume of the child in the final Miracle scene should be white and he should be the only one so clad. Novices are also traditionally dressed in white. In the Miracle scene they can be kept somewhat in the background among the other nuns in order not to ruin the effect of the child's appearance.

Nuns' costumes (336) consisted of the 'habit,' a long-sleeved, ankle-length, loose-fitting garment, girdled at the waist by a white or off-white cord. Its loose ends, knotted at the bottom, hang down on one side. For outdoor purposes a cape matching the habit may be added. Its length varies. The 'scapula' which hangs from the shoulders is very frequently, but not always used. Its color often contrasts with the habit and it is never girdled. Its slenderizing faculties make it for theatrical purposes an invaluable accessory. The 'collar,' 'forehead band,' and the 'wimple' are always white. The latter which must fit tightly around the face also covers the ears. This can be a problem for singers who do not like to sing with their ears covered because it changes the way they hear the sound of their own voices, which may be profoundly upsetting to them. The section of the wimple which covers the ear may be replaced with a piece of coarse net to alleviate that problem. The tight fit around the face may be helped by cutting the fabric on the bias or by the use of a stretch fabric like jersey. Under no circumstances can the wimple be omitted. It is a very typical part of a nun's dress. A black nontransparent head veil, sometimes lined in white, covers the head. Its length varies with the importance of the wearer. Black ballet practice slippers and black hose are the standard foot covering, although sandals on bare feet have also been encountered.

The religious order to which the nuns in *Suor Angelica* belong is never mentioned. That gives the costumer leeway how to differentiate through the use and combination of colors and accessories between the various categories of nuns as they appear in the opera. In addition to the regular nuns these are: the Abbess, the Monitor, the Lay sisters, the Novices, the Nursing sister, and the Alms collectors.

The privilege of being dressed all in black remains best reserved for the Princess so long as the nuns are not also in black (337). The color and the rich quality of her garment's fabric should be in striking contrast to the nuns. She also wears a complementary hat.

Illus. 336

Illus. 337.

Illus. 338

The appearance of the statue of The Virgin (338) should have the aspects of a statue come to life with all the Baroque glamour of such statues. If in fact a real statue could be constructed with one movable arm with which to push the child towards Angelica, the effect would be indeed miraculous!

GIANNI SCHICCHI

The year 1299 in which the events of *Gianni Schicchi* have occurred should not restrict the costumer's imagination too much. So long as the opera visually breathes the atmosphere of the early Renaissance times, a few years more or less will not matter so long as it will help the entire cast in their efforts at characterization.

The Donati's clothes should give the impression that its wearers have seen better times. To achieve a faded worn look that will carry across the footlights requires some special treatments of spraying, bleaching, etc. If the costumes come from rental stock, it may be possible to find some already in that ostentatiously worn state. They must not all be equally conditioned that way, however. Betto (339) is the poorest among them. Even the libretto mentions that he is in rags. He also seems to have kleptomaniacal tendencies. His long-faded robe has therefore long ample sleeves with ragged edges in which he manages to conceal whatever he steals. The robe also has straight, but loose undersleeves. A scapula with hidden pockets on the inside will help to hide from view the silver platter he appropriated but which eventually crashes to the floor. If the bottom of the pocket is loosely sewn with a string, Betto can pull it surreptitiously and thus cause the platter to fall. He can wear a skullcap on his straggly greyish blond hair and sport an equally sparse mustache and beard.

Simone is the oldest as we are told again and again. He is even older than Zita, whose official title is: The Old Woman. Furthermore he has been the mayor of Fucecchio, as his relatives keep reminding him, wherefore his dark long robe should have an air of dignity. A hooded cowl with a fur-edged scalloped hem and hanging sleeves equally scalloped and fur-edged, may just supply that air of dignity, together with a bald pate fringed with half-long white hair and a voluminous white beard and mustache.

Zita comes across as a shrivelled up, shrewd old lady, who gives a somewhat nun-like impression and may well be in black, for she is

Illus. 339

no doubt in mourning for some relative or another. Her white headdress, however, should not be like that of a nun.

La Ciesca and Marco are a married couple as are Nella and
Gherardo, who furthermore have a seven-year-old son, Gherardino. It
would be helpful if color-wise these relationships could be reinforced,
for otherwise it is difficult to know who belongs with whom. Marco
might wear a dark blue tunic trimmed in light blue, a light blue
turban-like hat and matching tights, while La Ciesca may wear a light
blue gown with dark blue accessories and headdress. The same
method in dark and light green might be followed for Gherardo and
Nella, while little Gherardino should do well in a light and dark green
mi-parti tunic and tights, plus a little fez.

Rinuccio (see 339) and Lauretta's costumes (see 339) must relate,
of course. Of all the Donati his should be the least shopworn, while
hers must be attractively simple and unadorned, including her hairdo.

That Schicchi was born a peasant does not imply that he will go
through life looking and behaving like one, since he evidently worked
his way up by his considerable wits. On the contrary, he may not want
to be reminded of his background, especially since he envisions a
marriage up the social ladder for his daughter Lauretta. It is important
to consider that Schicchi will have a change of costume in full view of
the audience. Later on, that costume will be ripped off him under the
same conditions. He must, therefore, be presentable, dressed or undressed. The best solution for that problem is a unicolored longsleeved
leotard (340), which will cover all eventualities. Over the leotard he
wears a matching, belted, knee-length, fur-trimmed tunic of a far
richer fabric (341), with hanging sleeves. If the tunic has a V neckline
right down to the belt, the simple opening of the belt buckle will make
for that garment's easy removal, while taking off his hat which
consists of a fur roundlet and liripipe, will present no problems. Here
then stands Signor Schicchi in all decency in his leotard, ready to don
Buoso Donati's night shirt, chinband, and night cap (342). The
function of the chinband (in Italian 'pezzolina' (343), meaning a small
piece of linen) is not always understood. Passing under the chin and
tied on top of the head underneath the night cap, it served to prevent
the chin of a dead person from sagging and hence the mouth from
opening. The easiest way to put on the night shirt is for it to be open
in the middle back and get closed there with a few velcro tabs. A
foolproof method of dealing with the ripping off process is to have the
garment pre-torn and basted back together again with large loose

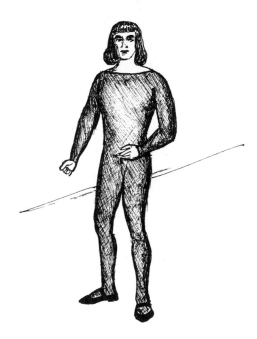

TOP, LEFT: Illus. 340; BOTTOM, RIGHT: Illus. 341.

stitches. Aside from avoiding the need for a new night shirt at every rehearsal and performance, it also insures that the garment will rip at the most visually appropriate places or prevents, heaven forbid, the fabric from refusing to tear at the crucial moment.

Master Spinelloccio, the physician, wears a black ankle-length robe with three-quarter-length-wide sleeves, over fitted undersleeves. A 'Dante' type headdress is suitable for him and he may carry the 14th-century equivalent of a doctor's bag.

Amantio di Nicolao is similarly dressed in a robe of dark red accompanied by a purple roundlet and liripipe.

Master Pinellino the shoemaker put on a leather apron over his hooded cloth tunic and tights, while Master Guccio the dyer wears, true to his profession, a blotchy multicolored shirt, and two-tone tights.

Felt and leather slippers which can be dyed, sprayed or covered will solve the men's shoe problems, while the ladies do best in ballet practice slippers, which can be processed in the same manner. Heels are out for the duration!

Illus. 342.

Illus. 343.

CHAPTER *15*

MOZART'S

Die Zauberflöte

*T*HE CONCEPT ADOPTED FOR a theatrical production includes per force its visual elements. It should be no different in the case of *Die Zauberflöte,* but pictures of its productions through the ages do not bear out this contention. From the very outset the opera's visual aspects have been a 'mish-mash.' The term is used advisedly for in the volumes that have been written about the opera's libretto, its background, and the circumstances that caused it to evolve into its final form, the expression 'mish-mash' occurs again and again. Only to the music does this term not apply, for although Mozart gave each character its own musical identity, he created at the same time a musically unified totality.

In the best sense of the word Mozart was a man 'possessed.' Within the limits he set himself of what was acceptable, he would write music for almost any purpose or occasion. In the realm of vocal music that encompassed: 'Opera Seria,' 'Singspiele,' 'Children's

310

songs,' 'Religious music,' 'Masonic music,' . . . . you name it, and he would be glad to oblige. Mozart's genius is *Die Zauberflöte*'s saving grace.

In this chapter, wherein the costumer propounds his views regarding the opera's costume requirements one assumes that these views are in accordance with a concept agreed upon in advance for the visual aspects of the entire production.

The Masonic Fraternity, which had its origins in medieval times among the Guilds of Masons, derived much of its symbolism from ancient Egypt. It is not strange, therefore, that the scenes in the opera which occur in Sarastro's palace take place in Egypt. Where the mythical realm of the Queen of the Night exists is never made clear, but it is evidently within walking distance of Egypt, because the border between the two is being crossed constantly as the action proceeds. Of the few subjects of the Queen of the Night with whom we get acquainted, her daughter Pamina is the only character with a more complex personality. The three Genii are also mythical creatures although they are world wise and have common sense. Their odd change of allegiance from the Queen to Sarastro shows that they know which side their bread is buttered on. There is nothing mythical about the Queen's three Ladies in Waiting, however. Papageno, who seems to have feathers in his head as well as on his costume, is not an unrealistic character, limited though his outlook may be. Prince Tamino is on the same wavelength as Pamina. His Japanese origin must be taken with a grain of salt. That Sarastro invented Papagena, as well as her disguise, shows that he has a sense of humor which is nowhere else apparent in his demeanor. The many people of his entourage seem pretty sober as well, not to say stodgy, except Monastatos who is mean and lusty.

By the middle of the 18th century a gradual change had taken place in the visual aspects of theatre productions, including opera (chapter-opening illustration, 344). Until then these had been exceedingly stylized undertakings which put great emphasis on spectacular presentation regardless of the subject matter. Eventually the need for greater realism was felt, and its impact became increasingly apparent. The burden of combining these elements in a sensible manner is, in this case especially, the producer's arduous task. There is the danger of an approach which singles out one character to set the tone for the entire production. This was done in the Swedish film version of the opera, which approached everything from Papageno's point of view.

Illus. 344a.

The priests, for instance, wore threadbare gloves, holes and all, which is entirely out of sync with their music. The only acceptable approach is the one Mozart adopted.

TAMINO

The 18th century's fondness for the exotic expressed itself in a preference for characters from faraway places be they Turkish, Chinese, African, Oriental, Albanian, or whatever. Having decided that Tamino's alleged Japanese origin is to be regarded in that vein, a modified Baroque interpretation of a male leading man's costume is in order for him (344a). He is making a tour of foreign countries before succeeding his father to the throne, as was the custom for young princes. Hence he is in travelling clothes. A decorated leather jerkin with shoulder puffs, tight sleeves, and breeches will fill that purpose. A matching shoulder cape will serve as a good travel companion. A pleated ruffle at the neck and wrists is appropriate, as well as complementary hose and leather shoes. There is an intentional slight mixture of periods here, which will be pursued throughout, in keeping with the style of the libretto. During the trial Tamino's head is covered by a veil. The libretto describes the royal couple's final attire as 'priestly robes,' which seems inappropriate. They do not become priests. Instead an ample white velvet armhole cloak, replacing the shouldercape, plus a matching beret, trimmed with a jewelled brooch and an ostrich feather, seems more suitable as the initiation garment for this young bridegroom (345).

PAPAGENO

Engravings of Papageno's costume as it was worn by Schikaneder in 1791 (346a) and in 1794 (346b), have been reproduced time and again. It is of interest to compare these with the way he is portrayed in the many mise-en-scène engravings of the 1794 production (347). In 1791 the costume seems to consist of a longsleeved jerkin with a long bird's tail, tights, and a collar, all of them covered with feathers. Those on the tights are noticeably different from those covering the jerkin. In the 1794 version he has lost his tail and the entire costume gives more the impression of a leotard covered with feathers. In the mise-en-scène pictures Papageno is

Illus. 345.

LEFT: Illus. 346a; RIGHT: Illus. 346b.

Illus. 347.

bareheaded in contrast with the costume engravings which reveal a rather substantial feather headdress. In subsequent productions through the ages, the costume has been stylized and modified. On occasion the feathers have even been omitted entirely. Papageno's sole reason for dressing in feathers is that in his endeavor to catch birds he tries to appear like one, which is wholly in keeping with his personality and there is no reason to change it. Instead of sewing individual feathers to a foundation, it is possible to purchase feather pads, which the millinery industry produces. It greatly facilitates the costume's construction. Although tailcoats had not yet seen the light of day in 1791, it would be awfully nice to supply Papageno with a feathered tailcoat, vest, breeches, tights, and skull cap. In moments of relaxation he could then remove the coat and still be properly feathered. And may Isis and Osiris pardon the anachronism. The colors of the feather pads and their distribution depend naturally on the production's overall color scheme, but they should be brightly hued.

MONASTATOS AND THE SLAVES

Monastatos is a 'Moor,' in German: 'Mohr' a word that various dictionaries define differently. 'Blackamoor' is the term that applies to him, for he himself refers to his dark skin, which is the cause of his problems with the fair sex. African characters were popular in Baroque opera but their costumes were traditionally of the 'Turkish' genre (348). So it shall be for Monastatos as well, who wears short Turkish pants, a bolero, a full-sleeved collarless shirt, a waist sash, and a turban (349). Although Monastatos is one of Sarastro's many slaves, he seems to be a few notches above the others, which is evident through some ornamentation along the edges of his bolero, and a more prominent sash and turban than those worn by the other slaves, who are otherwise in dress identical to him and each other. They all wear sandals. Interestingly, in the cast list of the opera's original playbill Monastatos is listed only as: 'Ein Mohr,' without defining his status further.

THE GENII

The first time the Queen's three Ladies mention the Genii, they refer to them as 'boys,' who will "float about you on your voyage,"

TOP, LEFT: Illus. 348; BOTTOM, RIGHT: Illus. 349.

which means that in deus ex machina fashion, they moved about the stage suspended on a cloud (350). After switching their allegiance to Sarastro, without so much as 'by your leave,' the libretto merely mentions that they 'enter,' as if they are on foot. Since it is theatrically no longer fashionable to travel on clouds and remains technically very costly, it will be assumed that they are indeed on foot (351). (This writer witnessed a production in which they were occasionally peeking through the leaves in trees, which was very effective.) Whether the roles of these unearthly creatures are interpreted by real boys or by women, naturally has some bearing on their costumes because in the latter case some female attributes will have to be disguised. Something surreal is desirable in any event. The libretto mentions that the Spirits (as they are also referred to) enter, holding silver palm branches in their hands. For this designer that is as good a clue for their costumes as any: Stylized silver palm leaves, over silver leotards can be adapted to make handsome Spirit costumes, while wreaths of palm leaves on their heads will be a suitable finishing touch.

SARASTRO AND THE PRIESTS

A part of the locale of Sarastro's palace is identified in the libretto as: 'a magnificent Egyptian room' (Act I, Scene 2). It is the only time Egypt is mentioned. In the Swedish film *The Magic Flute* (1974), Sarastro and the Queen of the Night were, at one time at least, husband and wife. If this were true there would be a bit of incest afoot, for Sarastro would then be in love with his own daughter. That he is in love with her he states very simply in two sentences as he says to her: "You love another very much" and "I cannot force you to love, but I will not grant you freedom." Sarastro is evidently suffering from the same syndrome which would beset, many centuries later, Don Alfonso in *Cosi fan tutte,* Dr. Malatesta in *Don Pasquale,* and Hans Sachs in *Die Meistersinger Von Nuernberg.* They are all aging bachelors who have to face the reality that as love objects they are no longer in the running. In the process of coming to terms with this fact of life they put some obstacles in the way of the young lovers.

As the High Priest of Isis and Osiris, Sarastro can be expected to wear an Egyptian priest's costume. Unfortunately, the antique Egyptian styles do not lend themselves well for this purpose. Baroque adaptations of Assyrian costumes (352, 353) will fit the situation far

TOP, LEFT: Illus. 350; BOTTOM, RIGHT: Illus. 351.

better. Sarastro is clad in a long ample robe with long, medium wide sleeves of gold cloth. The other priests wear the same robes, less lavish in cut and off-white in color. Sarastro wears in addition a full-length ample armhole cloak, which may be of a darker gold fabric. Decorations of Masonic emblems may be freely applied to these robes. Modified versions of the armhole cloak will serve the Speaker and the First and Second Priests as well. The flat-topped conical headgear of the Assyrians, embellished with Masonic symbols, is also suitable for the long haired, bearded Sarastro and in a simpler version for his fellow priests (354). Their footwear consists of sandals.

THE MEN IN ARMOR

The 'Men in Armor' are evidently Temple Guards. Egyptian sources supply little that agrees with our concept of 'Men in Armor.' A far more satisfactory solution is found among Assyrian costumes which reveal helmeted men wearing belted, ankle-length chainmail tunics, which will serve the purpose perfectly (355).

THE THREE LADIES

To this listener the music and the text of 'The Three Ladies,' presumably Ladies in Waiting to the Queen of the Night, portray three biddies. Papageno is correct in his conclusion that they are veiled because of their lack of beauty. The audience has a chance to convince itself of this, for upon their first entrance they are not veiled.

The best silhouette to be adopted for their gowns is that which ruled theatrical presentations (356) for a long time until the advent of the rococo panier. One reads on occasion that the ladies are dressed in black, which makes no sense. Only women in mourning wore black, and so far as we know the three ladies are not in mourning. A bluish-grey velvet, trimmed in silver is a good choice for them, since it will harmonize with the Queen in a subdued manner. They wear appropriate headdresses, and if the veils are long enough in front, they can be lifted over the headdresses to reveal their aging features.

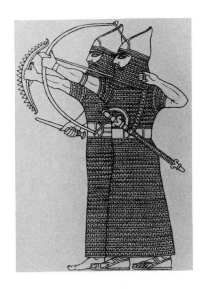

TOP, LEFT: Illus. 352; TOP, RIGHT: Illus. 353; BOTTOM, LEFT; Illus. 354; BOTTOM, RIGHT: Illus. 355.

THE QUEEN OF THE NIGHT

Although Pamina makes it plain that she truly loves her mother, the Queen of the Night seems to have few appealing characteristics. Whereas her rage in the second aria is genuine, her tears in the first one seem to be of the crocodile variety. There is no doubt, however, that she is an imposing, nay, even awe-inspiring figure. Her voluminously skirted baroque style gown (357) of midnight blue brocade has a considerable train. It is richly decorated with swirling bands of gold stars, which graduate in size from large at the hem to small at the waist. These also adorn the tight-fitting bodice and voluminous over sleeves, not to mention her imposing star-shaped tiara and veil. Her costume for the second aria is in various shades of flame colors (358). It displays a certain organized disarray in order to convey the fury she unleashes. She will return to the first costume for her final appearance, adding an ample cape of midnight blue- and dark gold-organza, which will underline her ensuing fate of doom and eternal destruction.

PAMINA

Pamina is the only multi-faceted character in the opera. She is not only pure and lovable, but also steadfast, faithful, mother loving, honest and suicidal. There is no way all these character traits can be expressed in one costume, where youth and purity must prevail. The silhouette of her gown (359) is no different than that of the other women, save for a somewhat less voluminous skirt and one less petticoat as a tribute to her youth. Its color, if not white or off-white, must be a very light one. If the figure of the singer cast to execute Pamina's taxing music requires some slenderizing features the bodice of her costume may be split in front to reveal a stomacher, while the skirt can be parted in similar fashion to uncover the underskirt. A modest tiara will suffice for her and after the successful completion of the trials, she too is given a full-length white armhole cloak as a token of her initiation, rather than priestly robes. A flowered wreath and veil will thus proclaim her a happy bride.

PAPAGENA

Papagena wears a female version of Papageno's costume (360). It is suggested, however, that only her bodice, apron, and mob cap be

TOP: Illus. 356; BOTTOM, LEFT: Illus. 357; BOTTOM, RIGHT: Illus. 358.

made of feathers. Her calf-length skirt is made of a lightweight fabric in a light, complementary shade. Light green seems a good choice. Papagena's old hag disguise (361) consists of an ample, fairly dark and drab-colored, hooded cape. The latter will hide her youthful features. Some grey hair sewn into it, as well as a half mask, can render the disguise even more surefire. The Spirits' utterance: "Now Papageno turn around!'' indicates that when they return with Papagena, still in her disguise, his back is turned to them. This gives her the opportunity to remove the cape and emerge as the youthful Papagena. Technically, the cape's borders must overlap enough to ensure a complete cover-up. A velcro fastening at the neck region will then suffice for a 'one fell swoop' transformation!

THE FEMALE CHORUS

One of the many surprises in the score of *Die Zauberflöte* occurs in the finale, when for the first time in the opera the chorus includes female voices. Who these women are is anybody's guess. It is unlikely that this sexist libretto would suddenly produce female priestesses. They may be boy-soprano priests, or women dressed as male priests. In either case they would be robed like all the other priests. One other possibility is that they are female servants, or 'slaves' as their male counterparts are billed. In that event long-sleeved robes, revealing Turkish pants underneath, would be worn (362). The familiar Oriental female headcovering, which only permits the eyes to be visible, should here be modified to bare the mouths as well, in order for these ladies to be audible.

THE ANIMALS

There are various ways of dealing with the animals who dance to Tamino's tune. Modern stage techniques enable the lighting designer to project them successfully. If there happens to be a circus around the corner, or another organization that specializes in training animals to perform, one can avail oneself of their services. Otherwise human beings, preferably children, will have to don animal suits and masks and go through the motions. A touch of humor in their attire and their performances will not be amiss.

TOP: Illus. 359; BOTTOM, LEFT: Illus. 360; BOTTOM, RIGHT: Illus. 361.

Illus. 362.

GLOSSARY

F = Female, M = Male

Aiguilette: A cord, partly braided, hanging at one shoulder and around the armhole of a uniform or livery. The ends usually have metal tips. It is worn in a variety of ways.

Ancien régime: French for "the old order," especially the one in power before the French Revolution. The term is also applied to the mode of costuming of that era.

Ankle tights: Three-quarter-length tight pants, often with a strap under the foot, usually worn with boots or leggings.

Armhole cloak: In the sixteenth century, an ample, sleeveless, three-quarter-length coat, its fullness often set onto a yoke. Frequently trimmed with a large fur collar and lapels extending down the entire length of the coat. M

Baigneuse: Originally a bathing cap, as the name implies, it developed in the eighteenth century into an elegant indoor head covering. It had endless variations, each with its own name. F

Baldric: In the seventeenth century, an elaborate belt worn diagonally over one shoulder, to the waist and below. Sometimes it served as a sword belt. M

Bandoleer: *See* Baldric

Bata: An Andalusian woman's gown of the late nineteenth century, with a princess-line bodice to the hip and a full skirt with a train, covered with ruffles.

Bertha: From about 1830 to 1860, a collar or border around a gown's wide décolletage.

Bias cut: Fabric cut on the diagonal of the grain.

Bib apron: An apron attached in the middle front to a flat piece of the same fabric, which covers part of the bodice. It may have shoulder straps at the top edge or may be pinned to the bodice. F

Bicorn: A man's hat of which the brim is turned sharply upward at two sides. Late eighteenth and first quarter of the nineteenth century.

Bolero: A short jacket not reaching the waist, and usually not closing middle front. It can be with or without sleeves. M, F

Bolivar: A top hat with a spreading crown. First half of the nineteenth century. M

Box pleat: An inverted pleat.

Canions: In Elizabethan times, a garment covering the thighs. In the late seventeenth century, knee ruffles worn particularly with petticoat breeches. M

Capote: A small hat worn off the face and tied under the chin, popular in the "bustle" period. F

Caraco: In the eighteenth century, a hip-length garment with a "sack" back. F

Changeable fabric: A weave of which the woof is of a different color than the warp, resulting in an iridescent-looking fabric that will seem to change colors depending on where the light strikes it.

Chapeau: Short for "chapeau à bras," a tricorn or bicorn carried under the arm. Now a ceremonial bicorn, like an ambassador's.

Chapeau claque: Opera hat with a collapsible crown. M

Chemise dress: Late eighteenth-century dress omitting paniers and worn with a wide slash.

Chignon: A coil of hair at the nape of the neck. F

Circlet: A simple headband worn in ancient and medieval times. F, M

Clerical tabs: A rudimentary "falling band" worn with a cassock when not officiating. Eighteenth century.

Cockade: A rosette, usually decorating a hat. M, F

Coif: A linen head covering, medieval in origin. F, M

Congress gaiters: Ankle-high boots with an insert of elastic webbing at the ankle. Nineteenth and twentieth centuries. M

Court mantle: In Empire fashions, an elaborately decorated velvet train starting just below the bust and supported by halters.

Crested helmet: Of Greek-Roman origin, a military helmet with a raised section on the crown, often topped with feathers or a brush. Popular in the nineteenth century and still used by honor guards on ceremonial occasions.

Cross-belt: Two shoulder belts, one over each shoulder, crossing middle front and back over a uniform coat.

Cuff ruffle: In the late-seventeenth century and the eighteenth century, the shirt-sleeve protruding beyond the coat-sleeve's cuff. Frequently of lace. M and sometimes F for hunting coats.

Cuffietta: A soft indoor head covering, worn throughout the nineteenth century. F

Day cap: In the eighteenth century, a covering for the shaven skull in lieu of a wig. M

Dolman sleeve: A sleeve narrow at the wrist but with an exceedingly deep armhole, sometimes extending to the waist. F, M

Domino: An ample hooded masquerade costume, based on a monk's habit. F, M

Doublet: A tight-fitting, padded torso covering, worn during the fifteenth, sixteenth, and seventeenth centuries. M but occasionally F as a riding habit.

Dropped shoulder: Fashionable in women's dress of the 1830s, when the shoulder width was extended down the upper arm, thus narrowing the armhole and restricting the arm motion.

Empire hairstyles: Called "à la Titus." An imitation of ancient Greek and Roman hairstyles during the Empire period. F, M

Engageante: In the eighteenth century, a triple lingerie ruffle, facing and protruding beyond the sleeve's flounce, just below the elbow. F

Entre deux: A lace insert.

Espadrille: Spanish peasant's footwear with a rope sole.

Farthingale: A framework used in the sixteenth century to hold out a woman's skirt. French, Spanish, and English farthingales existed, each with a different silhouette. The one illustrated is the English "drum farthingale."

Fichu: A usually transparent triangular neckerchief covering a dress's décolletage.

Fillet: Man's headband in ancient Greece, worn by women in the eighteenth and nineteenth centuries.

Fontange: A high cap of lace or linen, trimmed with loops and supported by a wire frame. Late seventeenth century. F

Frogs: A looped coat fastening, made of braid or cord. F, M

Full-bottomed wig: Late seventeenth, early eighteenth century, curly shoulder-length wig, parted in the middle. M

Gaiter: A cloth or leather covering extending over the top of the shoe and around the ankle or higher. Usually with a strap under the instep. F, M

Gallooned: Trimmed with galloon, a decorative flat braid. M, F

Gauffering (Goffering): An intricate gathering of fabric, used in the nineteenth century on women's indoor caps, for example.

Gorget: A metal collar, part of the armor. M

Greaves: Greek and Roman soldiers' shin protectors, reaching from the ankle to the knee.

Halberd: Originally an ax on a long pole. Still used as a symbol of office, e.g., by the Vatican Swiss Guard.

Hanging cap: (Also bag cap or stocking cap.) A long, tubular head covering, gathered at one end and often finished with a tassel or a pompon.

Hanging sleeve: A loose oversleeve slashed to let the undersleeve come through. It appeared in many forms and lengths. Fifteenth, sixteenth, and seventeenth centuries. F, M

Hoover collar: A high, stiff, turnover collar. M

Horsehair tail: A switch of horsehair attached to the side or the top of a dragoon's helmet.

Incroyable: A fop of the French Revolution, boasting the elegance of ill-fitting garments.

Jabot: Originally a ruffle at either side of the neck opening of a man's shirt. The accepted men's neckwear throughout the eighteenth century. F also in the nineteenth century.

Jerkin: A close-fitting, short-skirted jacket, often sleeveless, worn in the sixteenth and seventeenth centuries. M

Justaucorps: Late seventeenth century. Man's close-fitting, long, square-cut coat.

Kilt: A wraparound, knee-length skirt. M

Lapel wig: *See* Full-bottomed wig

Legging: A cloth or leather leg covering of varying length. See gaiter. M, F

Leg-o'-mutton sleeve; A sleeve extremely full at the arm's eye, tapering toward the elbow, and tight at the underarm. 1830 and 1890. F, but in children's smocks also M.

Love lock: A lock of hair separated from the rest of the hairdo, to fall on the shoulder. Sometimes with a bow at the end. Seventeenth century. M

Medici cap: A widow's coif with a wired edge, named after Maria de' Medici. Seventeenth century. F

Merveilleuse: In the French Revolution, a woman's exaggeratedly careless dress, the female equivalent of an Incroyable.

Mi-parti: In medieval times, the geometrical color division of a garment, so that sections of one side are of different color than the corresponding section of the other side. Mostly M but occasionally F.

Mitten: 1. A glove without separate finger coverings except the thumb. F, M. 2. A dressy glove without fingers. F

Mobcap: An indoor head covering consisting of a circle of fabric shirred around the head a few inches from the edge, producing a puffed crown and a ruffled edge. Eighteenth century. F

Moiré: Watered silk.

Morion helmet: A crested, brimmed, sixteenth-century helmet, still worn today on ceremonial occasions by the Papal Swiss Guard.

Mousseline (Muslin, Mousselaine): A thin, soft, cotton fabric.

Norfolk jacket: A jacket (usually tweed) with two vertical bands front and back, underneath which a belt passes. M

Open seams: A peek-a-boo effect achieved by revealing the fabric of the underclothes through partly joined sections of the top fabric of the costume. Fifteenth, sixteenth, and seventeenth centuries. M, F

Opera gloves: Long, usually white gloves worn with a ball- or evening gown. Their length varied greatly at different periods.

Order sash: A grosgrain or moiré ribbon, part of a high-ranking decoration, worn across the chest on gala occasions. F, M

Ottoman: A ribbed silk fabric.

Padre shovel-hat: A low-crowned hat whose large brim is rolled up at the sides (but occasionally at the front and back). Worn by priests.

Pancake hat: A flat-brimmed, low-crowned hat. F

Paniers: Eighteenth-century side-hoops to extend the skirt's width.

Pelisse: A coatdress, originally fur lined. F

Peplum: A section of the bodice extending below the waist. F

Plastron: The superimposed front panel of a military coat, often of a contrasting color.

Plis Watteau: The pleats of a dress extending from the back of the neck and becoming part of the skirt. Eighteenth century.

Point d'esprit: Dotted net.

Poke bonnet: A hat with a stiff, off-the-face brim. Nineteenth century. F

Polonaise: A dress whose skirt has been pulled up in places (usually with inside tapes), revealing the underskirt. Eighteenth century.

Postiche: A false hairpiece. F

Pourpoint: A forerunner of the doublet. M

Prince Albert coat: A frock coat. M

Princess dress: A long, close-fitting dress cut in vertical panels. The skirt and bodice are not separated at the waist. Late nineteenth, early twentieth centuries.

Pumpkin hose: Short, puffed breeches. Sixteenth century. M

Puritan hat: A flat-brimmed hat with a conical crown. M, occasionally F.

Queue wig: A wig gathered at the nape of the neck with a bow or braided into a tail. Eighteenth century. M

Raffia: Fiber of the leaves of a palm tree, used for decorative purposes or woven into a strawlike material.

Reticule: A bag on a drawstring. F

Ruff: A heavily starched neck ruffle often supported by a wire frame. Second half sixteenth century and first half seventeenth century. M, F

Sack coat: A hip-length jacket. M

Schiller collar: An open-neck shirt collar. M

Self fabric: A trimming made of the same fabric as the garment it decorates.

Shako: Nineteenth-century military headgear with a cylindrical crown and often a visor brim.

Shantung: A China silk.

Shift: An undergarment worn next to the skin. F

Shirtwaist: A garment giving the appearance of a shirt but constructed like a dress bodice.

Sling cape: Short military jacket of a hussar's uniform, often fur edged, worn diagonally across the back like a shoulder cape.

Smoking cap: A pillbox hat worn with a dressing gown or a smoking jacket. Often trimmed with a tassel.

Snood: A net to catch long hair. M, F

Spats: *See* Gaiters

Square-cut coat: Long-skirted eighteenth-century coat. M

Steinkirk: Early eighteenth-century cravat, loosely tied, the end frequently pulled through a buttonhole.

Stick-up: An ornament at the top edge of a shako.

Stock: Nineteenth-century neckwear. M

Stocking cap: See Hanging cap

Stomacher: In the eighteenth century, a triangular piece of fabric, often lavishly decorated, pinned to the front of the corset. The gown's bodice was in turn pinned to the edge of the stomacher.

Straw boater: A stiff-brimmed straw hat with a flat-topped oval crown. F, M

Stuart collar: *See* Medici collar

Sunburst pleating: Fabric pleated on the diagonal of the grain, with each pleat starting exceedingly narrow at the top and gradually widening toward the bottom.

Surplice: A white linen or lace clerical garment worn during a service, over the cassock.

Swag: The front drape of a bustle skirt.

Sweetheart neckline: A décolletage starting close at the neck, then spreading outward and dipping toward the cleavage.

Swing tacking: A way of joining bodice and skirt with long, corded stitches on the inside of the garment.

Tabard: In the thirteenth and fourteenth centuries, an ample, wide-sleeved garment. M

Tailor-made: A woman's skirt and jacket made by a man's tailor following the principles of male tailoring.

Tiered shoulder cape: Several shoulder capes in rows of varying lengths on top of each other. F, M

Tonsure wig: An eighteenth-century clerical wig with a tonsure.

Tye-bag wig: A queue wig of which the tail is caught in a small rectangular bag, mainly for military. Eighteenth century. M

Visor helmet: A metal helmet that covered the entire head and often the neck as well. A hinged visor, perforated in order to permit vision and breathing, covered the face. The visor could be raised. The shape of helmet and visor varied widely. Fifteenth and sixteenth centuries. M

Weft: In wigmaking, a string to which strands of hair are attached.

Wing collar: A stand-up collar of which the middle-front corners have been folded back.

BIBLIOGRAPHY

Andersen, Ellen. *Danske Dragter, Moden i 1700 arene.* Copenhagen: National Museet, 1977.

Andersen, Ellen, and Bech, Viben. *Kostumer og Modedragte fra det Kgl. Teaters Herregarderobe.* Copenhagen: National Museet, 1979.

Anderson, Emily, ed. *The Letters of Mozart and His Family.* London: Macmillan & Co., 1938.

Angermueller, Rudolf. *Mozart, Die Opern von der Urauffuehrung his heute.* Berlin: Propyläen, 1988.

l'Avant Scene. *La Veuve Joyeuse.* Paris: Mensuel, 1982.

Barton, Lucy. *Historic Costume for the Stage.* Boston: Walter H. Baker Company, 1935.

Baur-Heinhold, Marga. *The Baroque Theatre.* New York: McGraw-Hill, 1967.

Beardsley, Aubrey, and Wilde, Oscar. *Salome.* New York: Dover Publications, 1967.

Belasco, David. *Madame Butterfly.* New York: Samuel French, 1935.

Benn, Christopher. *Mozart on the Stage.* London: Ernest Benn, 1946.

Berg, Inga Arnö, and Berg, Gunnel Hazelius. *Folkdraekter.* Vasteras, Sweden: ICA Bokfoerlag, 1975.

Berman, E., Kolinskov, V., and Kurbotovoye, E. *Ruskiy Kostyum 1750–1917.* Moscow: Vserosiyskoe Teatralynoe Obshchestvo, 1960.

Bestetti, Carlo, ed. *Abbigliamento e Costume nella Pittura Italiana, Barocco e Impero.* Rome: Edizione d'Arte, 1964.

———. *Rinacimento.* Rome: Edizione di'Arte, 1962

Beylie, Claude. *Lehar, La Veuve Joyeuse.* Paris: l'Avant Scene, 1982.

Bing, Valentyn, and von Ueberfeldt, Braet. *Nederlandsche Kleederdrachten.* Amsterdam: Frans Buffa & Zonen. 1857.

Blackie, Lorna. *Clans and Tartans.* New York: Gallery Books, 1987.

Boehn, Max von. *Biedermeier Deutschland von 1815–1847.* Berlin: Bruno Cassirer, n.d.

———. *England im 18 Jahrhundert.* Berlin: Askanischer Verlag, 1920.

———. *Die Mode.* Munich: Verlag F. Drueckmann, 1925.

Bory, Robert. *The Life and Works of Wolfgang Amadeus Mozart in Pictures.* Geneva: Les Editions Contemporains, 1948.

Boucher, Francois. *Histoire du Costume en Occident de l'Antiquite a nos jours.* Paris: Flammarion et Cie., 1965.

Braun, Louis et al. *Zur Geschichte der Kostueme.* Munich: Verlag Braun & Schneider, n.d.

Braun Ronsdorf, Margarete. *Des Merveilleuses aux Garconnes.* Paris: Editions des Deux Mondes, 1963.

Bruhn, Skarbina. *Kostuem und Mode.* Leipzig: L Stackmann Verlag, 1938.

Carrieri, Raffaele. *Imagini di Moda 1800–1900.* Milan: Editoriale Domus S.A., 1940.

Chailley, Jacques. *The Magic Flute, Masonic Opera.* trans. by Weinstock, Herbert. New York: Alfred A. Knopf, 1971.

Colle, Doriece. *Collars, Stocks, Cravats.* Emmaus, PA: Rodale Press. 1972.

Collie, George E. *Highland Dress.* Harmondsworth, England: Penguin Books Ltd., 1948.

Contini, Mila. *Fashion from Ancient Egypt to the Present Day.* New York: Odyssey Press, 1965.

Cornu, Paul. *Galerie des Modes et Costumes Françaises.* Paris: Librairie Centrale des Beaux Arts, n.d.

Cowles, Virginia. *The Romanovs.* Harmondsworth, England: Penguin Books, 1971.

Cunnington, C. Willet, and Cunnington, Phillis. *The History of Underclothes.* London: Michael Joseph, 1951.

Cunnington, C. W., Cunnington, P. E., and Beard, Charles. *A Dictionary of English Costume, 900–1900.* London: Adam and Charles Black, 1960.

Cunnington, Phillis, and Lucas, Catherine. *Costume for Births, Marriages, and Deaths.* London: Adam and Charles Black, 1972.

———. *Occupational Costume in England.* London: Adam and Charles Black, 1967.

Curtis International. *The Life and Times of Napoleon.* Philadelphia: Curtis Publications Co., 1965.

Davenport, Milia. *The Book of Costume, Vol I & II.* New York: Crown Publishers, 1948.

Dufresne, Claude. *Histoire de l'Operette.* Fernand Nathan. 1981.

Eaton, Quaintance. *Opera, a Pictorial Guide.* New York: Abaris Books, 1980.

Echagüe, Jose Ortizea. *España, Tipos y Trajes.* Madrid: Publicaciones Ortiz Echagüe, 1963.

Erté. *Costumes and Sets for "Der Rosenkavalier."* New York: Dover Publications, 1980.

Ferrero, Mercedes Viale. *La Scenografia. Vol. III.* Turin: Cassa di Risparmio, 1980.

Gammond, Peter. *The Magic Flute.* London: Barrie and Jenkins, 1979.

Gauthier, Maximilien. *Achille et Eugène Dévéria,* Paris: H. Floury, Editeur, 1925.

Gentlemen's Fashions. London: J. B. Bell, 1843.

George, M. Dorothy. *Hogarth to Cruikshank.* New York: Walker & Co., 1967.

Gernsheim, Alison. *Fashion and Reality.* London: Faber & Faber, 1963.

Gili, Gustavo. ed. *El traje Español en la epoca de Goya.* Barcelona: Editorial Gustavo Gili, 1962.

Griesebach, Edward. *E. T. A. Hoffmann, Saemtliche Werke.* Leipzig: Max Hesses Verlag. 1925.

Hackenbroch, Yvonne. *Meissen Porcelain.* Cambridge, MA: Harvard Univ. Pr., 1956.

Hamilton Hill, Margot, and Bucknell, Peter A. *The Evolution of Fashion.* London: B. T. Batsford, 1982.

Hammelmann, Hanns, and Osers, Ewalo, trans. *A Working Friendship, the Correspondence between Richard Strauss and Hugo von Hofmannstahl.* New York: Random House, 1961.

Hargreaves-Mawdsley, W. N. *A History of Legal Dress in Europe until the end of the 18th Century.* London: Oxford Univ. Pr., 1963.

Harter, Jim. *Women.* New York: Dover Publications, 1978.

Hartmann, Rudolf. *Richard Strauss, the Staging of his Operas and Ballets.* New York: Oxford Univ. Pr., 1981.

Hope-Wallace, Philip. *A Picture History of Opera.* London: Edward Hulton & Co. Ltd., 1954.

Houston, Mary C. *Ancient Egyptian, Mesopotamian and Persian Costume.* London: Adam and Charles Black, 1920.

Hughes, Patrick. *Famous Mozart Operas.* New York: Citadel Press, 1963.

Hutchings, Arthur. *Mozart, the Man, the Musician.* New York: Schirmer Books, 1976.

Imbourg, Pierre. *Van Dyck.* Monaco: Les Documents d'Art, 1943, 1949.

Janacek, Leos. *Letters and Reminiscences, Bohumir Stedron.* Transl. from Czech by Thomson, Geraldine. Prague: Artia, 1955.

Kahane, Eric. *Un Marriage Parisien sous le Directoire.* Paris: Editions le Carousel, 1961.

Kawakatsu, Ken-ichi. *Kimono* (Japanese Dress). Tokyo: Japan Travel Bureau, 1936.

Klimt, Gustav. *A Poster Book.* New York: Crown Publications, 1976.

Koslinskov, V., Berman, E., and Kurbatovoy, E. *Ruskiy Kostyum 1750–1917,* Moscow: Vserosiyskoe Teatralynoe Obshchestvo. 1960.

Kredel, Fritz, and Todd, Frederick P. *Soldiers of the American Army 1775–1954.* Chicago: Henry Regnery Co., 1954.

Kybalova, Ludmila, Herbenova, Olga, and Lamarova, Milena. *A Pictorial Encyclopedia of Fashion.* New York: Crown Publications, 1968.

La Croix, Paul. *France in the 18th Century.* New York: Frederick Ungar Publ. Co., 1963.

Langley Moore, Doris. *Fashion through Fashion Plates, 1771–1970.* New York: Clarkson Potter Inc., 1971.

Leloire, Maurice. *Dictionaire du Costume.* Paris: Librairie Grund, 1951.

MacKinnon, C. R. *Tartans and Highland Dress.* Glasgow and London: Wm. Collins Sons & Co Ltd., 1960.

Markov, Jozef. *The Slovak National Dress through the Ages.* Prague: Artia, 1956.

Martin, Linda. *The Way We Wore.* New York: Charles Scribner's Sons, 1978.

La Merveilleuse Histoire de l'Armée Francaise. Paris: Editions G.P., 1947.

Miller, William. printed for, *The Costume of Turkey.* London: Hewlett and Brimmer, 1804.

Moberly, R. B. *Three Mozart Operas.* London: Victor Gollancz, Ltd., 1967.

Mollo, John. *Military Fashion.* New York: G. P. Putnam's Sons, 1972.

———. *Uniforms of the Royal Navy.* London: Hugh Evelyn Ltd., 1965.

Mondadori, Periodici. (*I Grandi di tutti Tempi*) Goya. Milano: Mondadori, 1966.

Morgan, Agnes, ed. *Ingres Exhibition Catalogue.* Cambridge, MA: Fogg Art Museum, 1967.

Onassis, Jacqueline. ed. *In the Russian Style*. New York: Viking Press, 1976.

Osborne, Charles, *The World Theatre of Wagner*. New York: Macmillan, 1982.

Piton, Camille. *Le Costume Civil en France du XIII au XIX siècle*. Paris: Ernest Flammarion, 1926.

Pushkin, Alexandr Sergeyevitch. *The Queen of Spades*. London: The Folio Society, 1970.

Raymond, Walter H.T., ed., *Men's Wear, 75 Years of Fashion*. New York: Fairchild Publication, 1965.

Robida, A., and Toudouze, George G. *Francois Ier*. Paris: Boivin & Cie., 1909.

Rogers, Agnes. *Women Are Here To Stay*. New York: Harper & Brothers, 1949.

Rosenberg, Pierre. *Conservateur, Musée du Louvre: French Painting. The Age of Revolution, 1774–1830* (A Traveler's Exhibition). New York: The Metropolitan Museum of Art, 1975.

Rosenfeld, David. *Porcelain Figures of the 18th Century in Europe*. New York: Studio Publications, Inc., 1949.

Roulin, Dom. E. *Linges, Insignes et Vetements Liturgiques*. Paris: P. Lethielleux, 1930.

Rütz, Hans. *Wolfgang Amadeus Mozart*. München: Verlag C. H. Beck, 1950.

Sachs, Hannelore. *The Renaissance Woman*. New York: McGraw-Hill, 1971.

Schick, I. T. *Battledress*. Boston: Little Brown & Co., 1978.

Shaver, Ruth M. *Kabuki Costume*. Tokyo: Charles E. Tuttle Co., 1966.

Sinderbrand, Laura, curator. *The Undercover Story*. New York: Fashion Institute of Technology, 1983.

Sotkova, Blazina, and Smirous, Karel. *National Costume of Czechoslovakia.* Prague: Artia, n.d.

Squire, Geoffrey. *Dress & Society 1560–1970.* New York: Viking Press, 1974.

Stibbert, Frederick. *Civil and Military Clothing in Europe.* London: Benjamin Blom, 1968.

Trkanova, Marie. *Janacky Podle Vypraveni.* Prague: Pantheon, 1964.

Vaclavik, Antonin, and Orel, Jaroslav. *Textile Folk Art.* Trans. by Kazcerova, Helena. London: Spring Books, n.d.

Vicellio, Cesare. *Renaissance Costume Book.* New York: Dover Publications, 1977.

Wartmann, Wilhelm. *Honore Daumier.* Zurich, Switzerland: Manesse Verlag, Conzett & Huber, n.d.

Weigel, Hans. *Trachtenbuch.* Unterschneidheim, Germany: Verlag Walter Uhl., 1969.

Wendel, Friedrich. *Die Mode in der Karikatur.* Dresden, Germany: Paul Aretz Verlag, 1928.

Wilcox, R. Turner. *The Mode in Hats and Headdresses.* New York: Charles Scribner's Sons, 1948.

———. *R. Folk Festival Costume.* New York: Chas. Scribner's Sons, 1965.

Wildenstein, Georges. *The Paintings of J.A.D. Ingres.* New York: Phaidon, n.d.

Willet, C., and Cunnington, Phillis. *A Pictorial History of English Costume.* London: Longacre Press Ltd., 1960.

———. *Handbook of English Costume in the 18th Century.* London: Faber & Faber, 1964.

Wise, Terence. *Medieval Heraldry.* London: Osprey Publications Co., n.d.

SOURCES AND CREDITS

The number in front of of each listing corresponds with an illustration number in the text. An asterisk in front of the number or within a credit line or source note indicates a credit as dictated by the picture's source. All drawings are by Leo Van Witsen unless otherwise noted. All photographs not provided by museums or archives were taken by Earl Ripling.

Chapter 1: *Un Ballo in Maschera*

1. Sir Anthony Van Dyck, *Sir Thomas Wharton.* Hermitage Museum, St. Peterburg, Russia.
2. *Malmo Museum Catalogue.* Malmo Museum, Sweden.
3. Female National Costume. Nordiska Museet, Stockholm.
4. Chodowiecki illustration: "Delicieuse Creature" for Beaumarchais' *Le Mariage de Figaro,* Rijksmuseum-Stichting, Amsterdam.
5. See No. 2.
6. John Mollo. *Uniforms of the Royal Navy.* London: Hugh Evelyn Ltd., 1965.
7. Folkdräkter. ICA bökforlag. Västeras, Sweden, 1965. * Carl Lindhe, photographer.
8. T. Viero. Racolta I. *Legal Dress in Europe.* London: Oxford Univ. Pr., 1963.
9. Pehr Hillerström, Slatterölet pa Svartjö Slott. Nordiska Museet, Stockholm.
10. See No. 7.
11. See No. 7.
12. See No. 7.
13. Pietro Rotari, *Ritratto di fanciula.* Private Collection. Carlo Bestetti. *Abbigliamento e Costume nella Pittura Italiana. Barocco-Empero.* Rome: Edizione d'Arte, 1964.
14. Racolta della Stampe. Achille Bertarelli, Milan.
15. Pompeo Batoni, *Ritratto di giovane gentiluomo.* Museum of Fine Arts. The Samuel H. Kress Collection, Houston, Texas.
16. Camille Piton. *Le Costume Civil en France du XIII au XIX siècle.* Paris: Editions Flammarion, 1926.
17. Drawing by Francesca Mabon.
18. Johann Georg Lederer, *A Masked Ball in Bohemia* (detail) 34.83.2 Metropolitan Museum of Art, New York. Photog. Serv. Neg. 97000 TF.E.
19. Scuolo Veneziana. La sala del ridotto (part.) Venezia Museo Civico Correr.
20. Livrust Kammaren. Statens Konstmuseer, Stockholm.

Chapter 2: *Madama Butterfly*

21. Kimono. Tourist Library. Japan Travel Bureau.
22. Drawing by the author.
23. See No. 22.
24. Walter H. T. Raymond, ed. *Mean's Wear, 75 Years of Fashion.* New York: Fairchild Publications, 1965.
25. See No. 24.
26. Drawing by the author.
27/28. The World of Meiji Print. Metropolitan Museum Costume Library, New York.
29. See No. 27/28.
30. Drawing by the author.
31. Ruth M. Shaver. *Kabuki Costume.* Tokyo: Charles E. Tuttle Co., 1966.
32. See No. 31.
33. See No. 27/28.
34. See No. 21.
35. Drawing by the author.
36. Archives. Metropolitan Museum Costume Library, New York.
37. See No. 36.
38. See No. 21.
39a/b. See No. 31.
40a/b. See No. 31.
41. Drawing by the author.
42. See No. 27/28.
43a. Visions of Old Japan. Metropolitan Museum Costume Library, New York.
43b. See No. 31.
44. See No. 43a.
45a. See No. 31.
46. Phillis Cunningham. *Costume in Pictures,* 1964 * Reproduced by permission of Macmillan Publishing Company from *Costume in Pictures* originally published by Studio Vista Publishers © 1964.
47. See No. 31.

Chapter 3: *Les Contes D' Hoffmann*

48. Drawing by the author.
49. Costumes Parisiens. Metropolitan Museum Costume Library, New York.
50. Skarbina Bruhn. *Kostuem und Mode.* Leipzig: L. Staackmann Verlag, 1938.
51. Drawing by Francesca Mabon.
52. A "Garrick." * Bayerisches Nationalmuseum, Prinzregentenstrasse, Munich.
53. Drawing by the author.
54. Drawing by the author.
55. See No. 49.
56. Enrico Bandini, *Ritratto del cugino Tommaso Bandini.* Pinacoteca G. Stuarda. Parma, Italy.
57. Modes Parisiens. Metropolitan Museum Costume Library, New York.
58. Wm. Hogarth, *A Strolling Player, a 'Tragedy.'* * The Trustees of the British Museum. London.
59. * Historisches Museum der Stadt Wien.

60. Max von Boehn. *Biedermeier Deutschland von 1815–1847* Berlin: Bruno Cassirer Verlag, n.d..
61. Drawing by the author.
62. See No. 59.
63. See No. 59.
64. Fashionplate. Metropolitan Museum Costume Library, New York.
65. I. T. Schick, ed. Battledress. New York: Weidenfeld & Nicholson, 1978.
66. Antonio Canaletto: *La Novizza. Collocazione scenosciuta. Carlo Bestetti. Abbigliamento e Costume nella Pittura Italiana. Barocco e Imperio.* Rome: Edizione d'Arte, 1964.
67. Drawing by the author.
68. See No. 60.
69. Bunburry, *a Tragedy.* The Parker Gallery, London.
70. Modes de Paris. The Metropolitan Museum Costume Library, New York.
71. Andrea Appiani, *Ritratto di Ugo Foscolo.* Pinacoteca di Brera. Milan.
72. Achille Deveria, *Française.* H. Floury, Editeur. Paris, 1927.
73. Petit Courier des Dames. Metropolitan Museum Costume Library, New York.
74. Achille Deveria, *La Malibran.* H. Floury, Editeur. Paris, 1927.
75. Costume Parisien. Editions de la Gazette des Beaux Arts. Raymonde See, Editeur. Paris, 1927.
76. *Courier des Dames.* Bertarelli Collection, Milan.
77. * Pierre Paul Prud' Homme: *Portrait of the Empress Josephine.* Musée du Louvre. Paris.

Chapter 4: *Die Entführung aus dem Serail*

78. Silhouette of Catharina Cavaliere by H. Loschenkol. * Historisches Museum der Stadt Wien.
79. Drawing by the author.
80. Scene from Haydn's L'Incontro Improviso. ca. 1775. Marga Baur-Heinhold. *The Baroque Theatre.* New York: McGraw-Hill, 1967.
81. Giacomo Pregliasco, *Armida 1804'* 5. Biblioteca Civica. Turin, Italy.
82. Westermann Foto. H. Buresch.
83. Hulton Picture Co., London.
84. Francisco Jose de Goya, *Painting of Javier Goya.* Coll. de Noailles, Paris.
85. William Miller. *The Costume of Turkey.* London: Hewitt and Brimmer, 1804.
86. Drawing by the author.
87. See No. 85.
88. See No. 85.
89. Drawing by the author.
90. Drawing by the author.
91. Drawing by the author.
92. Sebastien le Clerq, *Mme. Clairon as Idame in "l'Orphelin de Chine."* Marga Baur-Heinhold. *The Baroque Theatre.* New York: McGraw-Hill, 1967.
93. Drawing by the author.
94. Drawing by the author.
95. Drawing by the author.
96. See No. 85.
97. See No. 85.

Chapter 5: *Jenufa*

98. Drawing by the author.
99. Blazina Sotkova and Karel Smirous. *The National Costume of Czechoslavkia.* Prague: Artia, n.d.
100. Antonin Vaclavik and Jaroslav Orel. *Textile Folk Art.* London: Spring Books, n.d.
101. See No. 99.
102. Drawing by the author.
103a,b, c, d. See No. 99.
104. Rudolf Mrlian, ed. *Slovak Folk Art.* Bratislava, Czechoslovakia: Tatran, n.d.
105. See No. 100.
106. The Function of Folk Art. Metropolitan Museum Costume Library, New York.
107. See No. 100.
108. See No. 104.
109. See No. 99.
110. See No. 99.
111. See No. 100.
112. See No. 104.
113. See No. 99.
114. See No. 99.
115. See No. 100.
116. See No. 99.
117. See No. 99.
118. The Slovak National Dress. Artia. Prague. 1956.
119. See No. 99.
120. See No. 118.
121. See No. 118.
122. See No. 104.
123. See No. 104.

Chapter 6: *Lohengrin*

124. Terence Wise. *Medieval Heraldry.* * London: Osprey Publications Co., n.d.
125. Abaris Productions Ltd.
126. Dutch costume plate.
127. Louis Braun et al. *Zur Geschichte der Kostueme.* Munich: Verlag Braun & Schneider, n.d.
128. Drawing by the author.
129. See No. 128.
130. See No. 128.
131. Dutch costume plate.
132. See No. 131.
133. Drawing by the author.
134. Dutch costume plate.
135. Drawing by the author.
136. See No. 135.
137. See No. 135.
138. Drawing by the author.
139. See No. 127.
140. Terence Wise. *Medieval Heraldry.* * London: Osprey Publications Co., n.d.

141. Drawing by the author.
142. See No. 127.
143. Drawing by the author.
144a, b, c. Dutch costume plate.
145. Terence Wise. *Medieval Heraldry.* * London: Osprey Publications Co. n.d.
146. Dutch costume plate.
147. See No. 146.

Chapter 7: *Lucia di Lammermoor*

148. *The Clans of the Scottish Highlands.* Text by James Logan. Plates by Robert McIan. Rudolph Ackermann, London 1845-47.
149. Maurice Leloir. *Dictionnaire du Costume.* Paris: SPADEM & Librairie Gründ, 1951.
150. Max von Boehn. *England im 18 Jahrhundert.* Berlin: Askanischer Verlag, 1920.
151. George Collie. *Highland Dress.* Hammondsworth, England: Penguin Books, Ltd., 1948.
152. John Telfer Dunbar. *The Costume of Scotland.* London: Batsford Ltd., 1950.
153. Metropolitan Opera Archives, New York.
154. See No. 151.
155. See No. 152.
156. Christian Hesketh. *Tartans.* Sir Henry Raeburn: Sir John Sinclair of Ulbster. London: Weidenfeld and Nicolson, n.d.
157. See No. 148.
158. C.R. MacKinnon. *Tartans and Highland Dress.* Glasgow and London: Wm. Collins Sons & Co. Ltd., 1960.
159. See No. 158.
160 (1,2,3). See No. 158.
161a. See No. 158.
162. See No. 148.
163. C. Williams: *A Tenth Rejected.* 1824. * Trustees of the British Museum, London.
164. Drawing by the author.
165. See No. 150.
166. Max von Boehn: *Die Mode.* Munich: F. Drueckmann, 1925
167. Joseph Scots. *The Tailors' Cuttingroom.* London: Blackie & Son, 1850.
168. See No. 167.
169. Drawing by the author.
170. See No. 158.
171. See No. 158.
172. Drawing by the author.
173. *Gentlemen's Magazine of Fashion.* London: J.B. Bell, May 1, 1943.
174. Anonymous.
175. Drawing by the author.

Chapter 8: *Die Lustige Witwe*

176. Drawing by the author. Museum of the City of New York.
177. 'Evening American,' 1908.
178. Drawing by the author.

179. Friedrich Wendel. *Die Mode in der Karikatur.* Dresden, Germany: Paul Laretz Verlag, 1928.
180. Francisco Jose de Goya, *Marquis Caballero.* Szepmuveszeti Muzeum, Budapest.
181. l'Avant Scene. Paris 1982.
182. Walter H. T. Raymond, ed. *Men's Wear, 75 Years of Fashion.* New York: Fairchild Publications, 1965.
183. Agnes Rogers. *Women Are Here to Stay.* New York: Harper & Brothers, 1949.
184. Radio Times. Hulton Co., London.
185. See No. 183.
186. Doris Langley Moore. *Fashion Through Fashionplates.* London: Geo. Rainbird Ltd., 1949. (First American edition published by Clarkson N. Potter, Inc., New York, 1971.)
187a to f. R. Turner Wilcox. *Folk Festival Costumes.* New York: * Reprinted with permission of Charles Scribner's Sons, an imprint of Macmillan Publishing Company from *Folk Festival Costumes* by R. Turner Wilcox. Copyright © 1965 by R. Turner Wilcox.
188. Bulgarian Native Costumes. Mayka Eizkustvo. 1950.
189. See No. 188.
190. See No. 179.
191. See No. 179.
192. See No. 181.
193. Alison Gernsheim. *Fashion and Reality.* London: Faber & Faber, 1963.

Chapter 9: *The Queen of Spades*

194. Vaerosiskoe Teatralynoe Obshchestvo, Moscow.
195. Drawing by the author.
196. See No. 195.
197. See No. 195.
198. See No. 194.
199. See No. 194.
200. Jacqueline Onassis, ed. *In the Russian Style.* New York: Viking Penguin, Inc., 1976. Candace Fischer-Pench, photographer.
201. See No. 200.
202. See No. 194.
203. See No. 194.
204. See No. 194.
205. Francois Gerard, *Portrait of Larevelierre-Lepeaux.* Musee des Beaux Arts. Angers, France.
206. French Painting 1774–1830. The Age of Revolution. Copyright © 1975 by the Detroit Institute of the Arts and the Metropolitan Museum of Art, New York. Laneuville, Portrait of Barere de Vieuzac. ca. 1792.
207. Jean Auguste Dominique Ingres, *Le Duc d' Orleans.* Musee National du Chateau de Versailles.
208. Jean Auguste Dominiqye Ingres, *Charles Francois Mallet.* * photograph © 1992. Art Institute of Chicago. All Rights Reserved.
209. Gallerie des Modes et Costumes. Librairie Centrale des Beaux Arts.
210. Francois Henri Mulard, *Portrait of a Lady.* Kimbell Art Museum, Fort Worth, Texas.
211. See No. 194.
212. Drawing by the author.

213. See No. 194.
214. Drawing by the author.
215. Max von Boehn. *Die Mode.* Munich: F. Drueckmann, 1925.
216. See No. 194.
217. See No. 200.
218. See No. 200.
219. Joseph Scots. *The Tailor's Cuttingroom.* London: Blackie & Son, 1850.
220. See No. 219.
221. Girodet, *Portrait of an Indian.* Musée Girodet, Montargis, France.
222. Achille Deveria, *Rachel.* H. Floury. Paris, 1928.
223. Hypolite le Comte. Costumes de Theatre.
224. Louis C. de Carmontelle: *Pas de Deux de l'Opera Sylvie.* Bibliothèque de l'Arsenal, Paris.
225. See No. 223.
226. See No. 209
227. See No. 200.
228. See No. 194.
229. See No. 194.
230. See No. 200.
231. Drawing by the author.
232. Skarbina Bruhn. *Kostuem und Mode.* Leipzig: L. Stackmann Verlag, 1938.
233. Jean Auguste Dominique Ingres, *Portrait of Guillaume Guillon Lethiers.* * Pierpont Morgan Library, New York. 1977.56.
234. Jean Auguste Dominique Ingres, *Portrait of Charles Naudet.* Museum of Art. Rhode Island School of Design, Providence, Rhode Island.

Chapter 10: *Rigoletto*

235. Robida & Toudouze. François I. Boicine, Cie., Paris, 1905.
236. Drawing by the author.
237. * Paolo Fiammingo, *Der Planet Venus* (part.) Inv. Nr. 4880. Bayerische Staatsgemaldesämmlungen.
238. Hans von Aachen, *Portrait of a Young Man.* Nardoni Gallery, Prague.
239. * Moretti, *Ritratto di Gentiluomo.* Reproduced by courtesy of the Trustees of the National Gallery, London.
240. Tiziano, *Ritratto de Fabrizio Salvaresio.* Kunsthistorisches Museum der Stat Wein.
241. See No. 235.
242. Giovanni Battista Moroni, *Ritratto di Bartolomeo Dongo.* Metropolitan Museum, New York.
243. Giovanni Battista. Moroni, *Ritratto di Gentiloumo.* Pinacoteca Ambrosiana, Milan.
244. Passerotti: *Ritratto di uomo.* Gia Monaco Coll., privata.
245. Cesare Vicellio's *Renaissance Costume Book.* New York: Dover Publications, 1977.
246. Nicolo del'Abbate: *Ritratto di giovinetto.* Private collection, New York.
247. Drawing by the author.
248. Girolamo da Carpi: (attr.), *Ritratto di Gentildonna.* Städelsches Kunstinstitut. Frankfurt am Maim, Germany.
249. Church of S. Martino di Buonomini. Florence, Italy.
250. * Giambatista Magenza: *Ritratto di Ippolito Porto.* Museo Civico di Palazzo Chiericati. Comune di Vicenza.
251. Neroccio de Bartolomeo, *La Vestale Claudia.* National Gallery of Art. The Samuel H. Kress Collection, Washington, DC.

252. Hans Weigel. *Trachtenbuch.* Unterschneiden, Germany: Verlag Walter Uhl, Germany, 1969.
253. Lucas Cranach the Elder. Szepmuveszeti Muzeum, Budapest.
254. See No. 252.
255. See No. 252.
256. See No. 252.
257. Drawing by the author.
258. Jim Harter. *Women.* A Pictorial Archive from 19th Century Sources. New York: Dover Publications Inc., 1978. Copyright free.
259. Pontormo: *Ritratto d'Ugolino Martelli.* National Gallery of Art. The Samuel H. Kress Collection, Washington, DC.

Chapter 11: *La Rondine*

260. Merveilleuses aux Garçonnes. Editions des Deux Mondes. Paris. Dr. Karl Grueber, Munich, photographer.
261. See No. 260.
262. Museum of Modern Art. New York. Film Library.
263. William Paxton: *Tea Leaves.* Metropolitan Museum Costume Library, New York.
264. Phillis Cunnington and Catherine Lucas. *Occupational Costume in England.* Dickens Pickwick Papers: Parlor Maid. G. Cruikshank. London: Adam & Charles Black Ltd., 1967.
265. Walter H. T. Raymond, ed. *Men's Wear, 75 Years of Fashion.* New York: Fairchild Publications, 1965.
266. See No. 265.
267. See No. 265.
268. See No. 265.
269. Drawing by the author.
270. Drawing by the author.
271. Max von Boen. *Die Mode.* Munich: F. Drueckmann, 1925
272. See No. 265.
273. See No. 271.
274. See No. 271.
275. See No. 263.
276. See No. 265.

Chapter 12: *Der Rosenkavalier*

277. Alfred Roller: *Baron Ochs.*
278. Erte. *Baron Ochs:* Sevenarts Ltd., London.
279. Lucy Barton. *Historic Costume for the Stage.* Boston: Walter H. Baker Co., 1935.
280. See No. 279.
281. See No. 279.
282. Galerie des Modes et Costumes. Librairie Centrale des Beaux Arts, Paris.
283. Drawing by the author.
284. See No. 282.
285. Drawing by the author.
286. Attr. to Henry Walton, *The Duke of Grafton.* * National Museums and Galleries on Merseyside. Walker Art Gallery, Liverpool.

287. Maurice Leloir. *Dictionnaire du Costume*. Paris: SPADEM. & Librairie Grund, 1951.
288. Wm. Hogarth, *Marriage a la Mode*. Metropolitan Museum Costume Library, New York..
289. See No. 288.
290. Wm. Hogarth. Metropolitan Museum Costume Library, New York.
291. See No. 288.
292. See No. 288.
293. Nicolas Lancret, Scene from "Le Glorieux." Deutsches Theatermuseum, Munich.
294. See No. 288.
295. * Photograph: Mydtskov. Det Kongelige Teater, Arkiv og Bibliotek. Copenhagen.
296. Det Kongelige Teater, Arkiv og Bibliotek. Copenhagen.
297. See No. 296.
298. Pompeo Battoni, *Ritratto di Nicolo Soderino*. Museo Pallazzo Vitelleschi. Tarquinia, Italy.
299. Vicountess Cremorne. Lieut. Comm. C. Windham.
300. C. Willet and Phillis Cunnington. *Handbook of English Costume in the 18th Century*. Portrait of a Lady by Thomas Hudson. Bristol City Art Gallery. London: Faber & Faber Ltd., 1957.
301. Women Are Here to Stay. Metropolitan Museum Costume Library, New York.
302. Drawing by the author.
303. See No. 287.
304. Allesandro Longhi, *Ritratto di Angelo Memmo*. Museo Civico Correr, Venice.
305. Drawing by the author.
306a. Antonio Cifrondi. Coll. Gregorio Scilitan, Milan.
306b. * Giacomo Ceruti. Padarello. Brescia. Coll Sal Va Dego.
306c. * Giacomo Ceruti. Padarello. Brescia. Coll Sal Va Dego.
307. Camille Piton. *Le Costume Civil en France du XIII au XIX siècle*. Paris: Ernest Flammaron, 1926.
308. Anton R. Mengs, *Ritratto di Nicolo Soderino*. Museo Pallazzo Vitelleschi. Tarquinia, Italy.
309a. Jean-Jacques de Boissieu, *La Danse des Enfants*. Musée du Petit Palais, Paris.
309b. Max von Boehn. *England im 18 Jahrhundert*. Berlin: Askanischer Verlag, 1920.
310. Drawing by the author.
311. George Romney, *Portrait of Mrs. Wilbraham Bootle*. * National Galleries of Scotland.

Chapter 13: *Salome*

312. Aubrey Beardsley and Oscar Wilde. *Salome*. New York: Dover Publications, 1967.
313. Gustave Moreau, *the Apparition*. Harvard University Art Museums Cambridge, MA.
314. Gustav Klimt, *Salome*. Galleria d'Arte Moderna, Venice.
315. Mary Houston. *Ancient Greek Costume*. Cambridge, England: Adam and Charles Black, 1965.
316. Louis Braun et al. *Zur Geschichte der Kostueme*. Munich: Verlag Braun & Schneider, n.d.
317. See No. 316.
318. See No. 315.
319. Drawing by the author.
320. Philip J. Watson. *Costumes of the Old Testament*. London, B.T. Batsford Ltd., n.d.

321. See No. 320.
322. See No. 320.
323. See No. 316.
324. See No. 316.
325. See No. 316.
326. See No. 316.
327. Drawing by the author.

Chapter 14: *Il Trittico, Il Tabarro, Sour Angelica,* and *Gianni Schicchi*

328. Drawing by the author. Museum of the City of New York.
329. See No. 328.
330. See No. 328.
331. See No. 328.
332. See No. 328.
333. See No. 328.
334. Drawing by Bouchardon ca. 1740 of a girl with a barrel organ. "La peitite Marmotte" from a series: "Cris de Paris." Wolfgang Bruhn-Max Tilke. *A Pictorial History of Costume.* New York: Praeger, ca. 1950.
335. Drawing by the author.
336a. Louis Braun et al. *Zur Geschichte der Kostueme.* Munich: Verlag Braun & Schneider, n.d.
336b. See No. 336a
336c. See No. 336a.
336d. See No. 336a.
337. * Raffaele Carrieri, *Immagini Di Moda 1800–1900.* Editoriale Domus S.A. Milan. Dec. 1940. Grande Mantaglinda passegio 1865-66.
338. Drawing by the author.
339. * Giovanni di Paolo, *Paraidiso.* Metropolitan Museum of Art, New York. Rogers Fund 1906. 061046.
340. Drawing by the author.
341. See No. 340.
342. See No. 340.
343. * Honore Daumier, *Portrait of Fieschi.* Publ. Maness Verlag Conzett & Huber. Zurich, Switzerland. 1835. Abbey Art Series.

Chapter 15: *Die Zauberflöte*

344. Theatre Italien: *Harlequin Discovered in the Seraglio.* Marga Baur-Heinhold. The Baroque Theatre. New York: McGraw-Hill, 1967.
344a. Christopher Benn. *Mozart on the Stage.* London: Ernest Benn, 1946.
345. Hypolite Lecomte. Le Costume de Theatre.
346. left. La Flute Enchantee. Bibliotèque National. Departement de la Musique, Paris.
346. right. La Flute Enchantee. Musée de l'Opera, Paris.
347. Die Zauberfloete. Historisches Museum der Stadt Wien.
348. William Miller. *The Costume of Turkey.* London: Hewitt and Brimmer, 1804.
349. See No. 348.
350. Ippolito Mazzarino, *Gli Amori delusi da Amore.* 1688. Biblioteca di Brera. Milan.
351. Tommasso Borgonio, *FAMA, con il Po e le Ninfe.* 1681. Biblioteca Nazionale. Turin, Italy.

352. See No. 345.
353. Mary C. Houston. *Ancient Egyptian Costume.* Cambridge, England: Adam and Charles Black, 1965.
354. See No. 353.
355. See No. 353.
356. See No. 345.
357. See No. 345.
358. See No. 345.
359. See No. 345.
360. Drawing by the author.
361. See No. 360.
362. See No. 348.

ABOUT THE AUTHOR

LEO VAN WITSEN, a native of The Netherlands, received his training as a Fashion Designer in Berlin at the Schule Reimann and in Paris with Bernard & Cie. Until his departure for the United States he ran a fashion-design studio in The Hague. His theatre costumes there were for the Cabaret De Vuurpijl and the Fritz Hirsch Operetta Ensemble.

In the United States he designed the costumes for Orson Welles' production of *Danton's Death* and millinery for Lili Dache, Mme. Pauline, Lenore Kroll, and Harry Cooper. For 40 years he was the staff costume designer for the New England Opera Theater, later the Goldovsky Grand Opera Company. He served on the faculties of the Juilliard School, the Curtis Institute of Music, and the Berkshire Music Center. He was head of the Opera Department of the Brooks Van Horn Costume Company for 20 years. Adele Addison donated two concert gowns of his design to the Costume Museum in The Hague.

His translation, from Dutch, of *The Agony of Fashion* by E. Canter Cremers was published in 1980 by Blandford Press. His illustrations for *Bringing Soprano Arias to Life* by Boris Goldovsky and Arthur Schoep was published by G. Schirmer in 1973. His first volume *Costuming for Opera, Who Wears What and Why* was published originally by Indiana University Press in 1981.

Still on the drawing-board are: *A Costume Guide for Opera Students;* an opera-costume history: *Opera Couture;* and *Cut out to be a Diva,* paper cutouts of opera costumes.